NEW
Treasury of Christmas Recipes

From Your Favorite Brand Name Companies

BEEKMAN HOUSE

This edition published by:
Beekman House
Distributed by Crown Publishers, Inc.
225 Park Avenue South
New York, NY 10003

Manufactured in U.S.A.

8 7 6 5 4 3 2 1

ISBN: 0-517-03553-7

Library of Congress Catalog Card Number: 90-61499

Pictured on the front cover (*clockwise from top left*): Roasted Turkey with Savory Cranberry Stuffing (*page 48*), Festive Eggnog Cake (*page 85*), Fireside Punch (*page 15*), Triple Chocolate Squares (*page 68*), Fruit Burst Cookies (*page 69*), Lemon Cut-Out Cookies (*page 65*) and Snowballs (*page 65*).

Pictured on the back cover (*clockwise from left*): Christmas Ribbon (*page 41*), Merry Cranberry Bread (*page 31*) and Scandinavian Smörgåsbord (*page 4*).

> **Microwave ovens vary in wattage and power output; cooking times given with microwave directions in this book may need to be adjusted.**

NEW
Treasury of
Christmas
Recipes

From Your Favorite Brand Name Companies
❅ ❅ ❅

Appetizers & Beverages

Scandinavian Smörgåsbord

Makes 36 appetizers

36 slices party bread, crackers or flat bread
    Reduced-calorie mayonnaise or salad dressing
    Mustard
36 small lettuce leaves or Belgian endive leaves
 1 can (6½ ounces) STARKIST® Tuna, drained
    and flaked or broken into chunks
 2 hard-cooked eggs, sliced
¼ pound frozen cooked bay shrimp, thawed
½ medium cucumber, thinly sliced
36 pieces steamed asparagus tips or pea pods
    Capers, plain yogurt, dill sprigs, pimiento
    strips, red or black caviar, sliced green
    onion for garnish

Arrange party bread on a tray; spread each with 1 teaspoon mayonnaise and/or mustard. Top with a small lettuce leaf. Top with tuna, egg slices, shrimp, cucumber or steamed vegetables. Garnish as desired.

Preparation time: 20 minutes

Calorie count: 47 calories per appetizer. Garnishes are extra.

Hot Maple Toddy

Makes about 3 cups

1 to 1¼ cups whiskey
1 cup CARY'S®, VERMONT MAPLE
    ORCHARDS or MACDONALD'S Pure
    Maple Syrup
¾ cup REALEMON® Lemon Juice from
    Concentrate
    Butter and cinnamon sticks, optional

In medium saucepan, combine all ingredients except butter and cinnamon sticks. Over low heat, simmer to blend flavors. Serve hot with butter and cinnamon sticks if desired.

Microwave: In 1-quart glass measure, combine ingredients as above. Microwave on 100% power (high) 4 to 5 minutes or until heated through. Serve as above.

Kahlúa® & Eggnog

Makes about 8 servings

1 quart dairy eggnog
¾ cup KAHLÚA®
    Whipped cream
    Ground nutmeg

Combine eggnog and KAHLÚA® in 1½-quart pitcher. Pour into punch cups. Top with whipped cream. Sprinkle with nutmeg.

Microwave Hot Chocolate

Makes about 4 cups or 4 servings

4 cups milk
1 package (4-serving size) JELL-O® Pudding and Pie Filling, Chocolate or Chocolate Fudge Flavor
COOL WHIP® Whipped Topping, thawed (optional)
Chocolate curls (optional)

Pour milk into 2-quart microwavable bowl. Add pudding mix. Beat with wire whisk until well blended. Microwave on HIGH 5 minutes; whisk again. Pour into mugs. Top with whipped topping and garnish with chocolate curls, if desired.

Preparation time: 5 minutes
Cooking time: 5 minutes

"Glogg"

Makes about 3 cups or 4 to 6 servings

1 package (4-serving size) JELL-O® Brand Gelatin, any flavor
3 cups boiling water
1 cinnamon stick
6 whole cloves
3 orange slices

Dissolve gelatin in boiling water in 4-cup measuring cup. Add cinnamon stick, cloves and orange slices. Cover; let stand 5 minutes. Remove spices and oranges. Pour gelatin mixture into mugs; serve warm. Garnish with additional cinnamon sticks and clove-studded orange slices, if desired.

Preparation time: 5 minutes

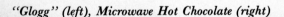

"Glogg" (left), Microwave Hot Chocolate (right)

Deviled Shrimp

Makes 4 to 6 appetizer servings

Devil Sauce (recipe follows)
2 eggs, lightly beaten
1/4 teaspoon salt
1/4 teaspoon TABASCO® pepper sauce
1 quart vegetable oil
1 pound shrimp, peeled and cleaned
1 cup dry bread crumbs

Prepare Devil Sauce; set aside. In shallow dish stir together eggs, salt and TABASCO® pepper sauce until well blended. Pour oil into heavy 3-quart saucepan or deep-fat fryer, filling no more than 1/3 full. Heat over medium heat to 375°F. Dip shrimp into egg mixture, then into bread crumbs; shake off excess. Carefully add to oil, a few at a time. Cook 1 to 2 minutes or until golden. Drain on paper towels. Just before serving, drizzle Devil Sauce over shrimp.

Devil Sauce

2 tablespoons butter or margarine
1 small onion, finely chopped
1 clove garlic, minced
1 1/2 teaspoons dry mustard
1/2 cup beef consomme
2 tablespoons Worcestershire sauce
2 tablespoons dry white wine
1/4 teaspoon TABASCO® pepper sauce
1/4 cup lemon juice

In 1-quart saucepan melt butter over medium heat; add onion and garlic. Stirring frequently, cook 3 minutes or until tender. Blend in mustard. Gradually stir in consomme, Worcestershire sauce, wine and TABASCO® pepper sauce until well blended. Bring to a boil and simmer 5 minutes. Stir in lemon juice. Serve warm over shrimp or use as a dip. Makes about 1 1/4 cups.

Celebration Punch

Makes 16 (6-ounce) servings

1 bottle (48 fl. oz.) DEL MONTE® Pineapple Orange Blended Juice Drink, chilled
1 can (46 fl. oz.) DEL MONTE® Apricot Nectar, chilled
1 cup orange juice
1/4 cup fresh lime juice
2 tablespoons grenadine
1 cup rum (optional)
Ice cubes

In punch bowl, combine all ingredients. Garnish with pineapple wedges and lime slices, if desired.

Torta California

Torta California

Makes 3 cups

2 8-oz. pkgs. **PHILADELPHIA BRAND®**
    Cream Cheese, softened
1 8-oz. pkg. goat cheese
1 to 2 garlic cloves
2 tablespoons olive oil
1 teaspoon dried thyme leaves, crushed
3 tablespoons pesto, well drained
⅓ cup roasted red peppers, drained, chopped

Line 1-quart souffle dish or loaf pan with plastic wrap. Place cream cheese, goat cheese and garlic in food processor or blender container; process until well blended. Add oil and thyme; blend well. Place one-third of cheese mixture in souffle dish; cover with pesto, half of remaining cheese mixture and peppers. Top with remaining cheese mixture. Cover; chill.

Unmold; remove plastic wrap. Smooth sides. Garnish with fresh herbs and additional red peppers, if desired. Serve with assorted crackers or French bread.

Preparation time: 15 minutes plus chilling

Fancy Ham-Wrapped Fruit

Makes 32 appetizers

1 (3-ounce) package cream cheese, softened
1 tablespoon orange marmalade
⅓ pound thinly sliced fully-cooked ham, cut into
    1×4-inch strips
2 papayas, peeled and cut into eighths
2 kiwifruit, peeled and sliced
1 orange (optional)

In a small bowl combine cream cheese and orange marmalade; mix well. Spread cream cheese mixture on one side of each ham strip. Place a piece of fruit on each ham strip and wrap ham around fruit. Cover and chill. To make orange peel garnish, peel orange in a long continuous strip about 1-inch wide. Roll into flower shape.

Preparation time: 20 minutes

Favorite Recipe from **National Pork Producers Council**

Oven-Fried Mushrooms

Oven-Fried Mushrooms

Makes about 24 appetizers

1/2 cup all-purpose flour
1/2 teaspoon paprika
1 cup soft bread crumbs
1/2 cup grated Parmesan cheese
2 teaspoons dried basil or oregano leaves,
  crushed
2 eggs, slightly beaten
2 tablespoons milk
1 package (16 ounces) **CAMPBELL'S FRESH®**
  mushrooms
1/4 cup butter or margarine, melted
  Dipping Sauce (recipe follows)

Preheat oven to 450°F. Lightly grease 15×10-inch jelly-roll pan. In plastic bag, combine flour and paprika. In another plastic bag, combine crumbs, cheese and basil. In small bowl, combine eggs and milk. Shake mushrooms in flour mixture and dip in egg mixture. Shake in crumb mixture, pressing crumb mixture to mushrooms to coat. Arrange mushrooms cap-side down on prepared jelly-roll pan. Drizzle with butter. Bake 10 minutes or until golden brown. Serve with Dipping Sauce.

Dipping Sauce: In small bowl, combine 1/4 cup mayonnaise, 1 tablespoon Dijon-style mustard or prepared horseradish and 1 tablespoon chopped fresh parsley. Makes 1/4 cup.

Tip: To prepare ahead, coated mushrooms can be covered and refrigerated until baking time.

Florentine Crescents

Makes 32 appetizers

1 10-oz. pkg. frozen chopped spinach, thawed,
  well drained
1/2 lb. **VELVEETA®** Pasteurized Process Cheese
  Spread, cubed
1/4 cup dry bread crumbs
3 crisply cooked bacon slices, crumbled
2 8-oz. cans refrigerated crescent dinner rolls

In 2-quart saucepan, combine spinach, process cheese spread, crumbs and bacon. Stir over low heat until process cheese spread is melted. Unroll dough; separate into sixteen triangles. Cut each in half lengthwise, forming thirty-two triangles. Spread each triangle with rounded teaspoonful spinach mixture. Roll up, starting at wide end. Place on greased cookie sheet. Brush dough with beaten egg, if desired. Bake at 375°F, 11 to 13 minutes or until golden brown.

Preparation time: 20 minutes
Baking time: 13 minutes per batch

Microwave: Combine spinach, process cheese spread, crumbs and bacon in 1 1/2-quart microwave-safe bowl. Microwave on High 2 1/2 to 4 1/2 minutes or until process cheese spread is melted, stirring every 1 1/2 minutes. Continue as directed.

Monterey Dipping Sauce

Makes about 3 cups

1 can (14 1/2 oz.) **DEL MONTE®** Stewed
  Tomatoes
1 can (8 oz.) **DEL MONTE®** Tomato Sauce
1/4 cup chopped onion
1 clove garlic, minced
2 tablespoons chopped fresh cilantro
2 teaspoons fresh lemon juice
1/2 teaspoon crushed oregano
1/4 teaspoon hot pepper sauce

Place stewed tomatoes in blender container. Cover and blend on medium 2 seconds. Combine remaining ingredients; stir in stewed tomatoes. Chill several hours. Serve as dip with shrimp or tortilla chips.

Carolers' Orange Cocoa

Makes 1 serving

1 envelope **ALBA®** Milk Chocolate Hot Cocoa
³/₄ cup boiling water
1 tablespoon orange-flavored liqueur
1 tablespoon frozen whipped topping, thawed
¹/₄ teaspoon grated orange peel

Empty **ALBA®** Hot Cocoa into mug or cup. Add water; stir until completely dissolved. Stir in liqueur. Top with whipped topping and orange peel.

Only 123 calories per serving.

Easy Sausage Empanadas

Makes 12 appetizer servings

1 (15-ounce) package refrigerated pie crusts
(2 crusts)
¹/₄ pound bulk pork sausage
2 tablespoons finely chopped onion
¹/₈ teaspoon garlic powder
¹/₈ teaspoon ground cumin
¹/₈ teaspoon dried oregano, crushed
1 tablespoon chopped pimiento-stuffed olives
1 tablespoon chopped raisins
1 egg, separated

Let pie crusts stand at room temperature for 20 minutes or according to package directions. Crumble sausage into a medium skillet. Add onion, garlic powder, cumin and oregano; cook over medium-high heat until sausage is no longer pink. Drain drippings. Stir in olives and raisins. Beat the egg yolk slightly; stir into sausage mixture, mixing well. Carefully unfold crusts. Cut into desired shapes using 3-inch cookie cutters. Place about 2 teaspoons of the sausage filling on half the cutouts. Top with remaining cutouts. Moisten fingers with water and pinch dough to seal edges. Slightly beat the egg white; gently brush over tops of empanadas. Bake in a 425°F oven 15 to 18 minutes or until golden brown.

Preparation time: 25 minutes
Cooking time: 15 minutes

Favorite Recipe from **National Pork Producers Council**

Apple Cinnamon Cream Liqueur

Makes about 1 quart

1 (14-ounce) can **EAGLE®** Brand Sweetened
Condensed Milk (NOT evaporated milk)
1 cup apple schnapps
2 cups (1 pint) **BORDEN®** or **MEADOW
GOLD®** Whipping Cream *or* Half-and-Half
¹/₂ teaspoon ground cinnamon

In blender container, combine ingredients; blend until smooth. Serve over ice. Garnish as desired. Store tightly covered in refrigerator. Stir before serving.

Fuzzy Navel Cream Liqueur: Omit apple schnapps and cinnamon. Add 1 cup peach schnapps and ¹/₄ cup frozen orange juice concentrate, thawed. Proceed as above.

Apple Cinnamon Cream Liqueur

Tangy Wisconsin Blue Cheese Whip

Makes about 2 cups

1 cup whipping cream
½ cup finely crumbled Wisconsin Blue cheese (2 ounces)
1 teaspoon dried basil, crushed
¼ teaspoon garlic salt
½ cup almonds, toasted and chopped
Assorted vegetable or fruit dippers

In a small mixer bowl combine whipping cream, Blue cheese, basil, and garlic salt. Beat with an electric mixer on medium speed until slightly thickened. Gently fold in chopped almonds. Serve with vegetable or fruit dippers. (Dip can be made ahead and chilled, covered, up to 2 hours.)

Preparation time: 15 minutes

Favorite Recipe from **Wisconsin Milk Marketing Board**©1990

Fresh Cranberry Frost

Makes 4 servings

1 cup ice water
2 envelopes ALBA® Vanilla Shake
1 cup fresh cranberries
½ teaspoon grated orange peel
12 large ice cubes

Pour water into blender container; add ALBA® Shake, cranberries and orange peel. Cover; process at low speed, adding ice cubes one at a time. Process at highest speed 60 seconds or until ALBA® mixture is thickened and ice cubes are completely processed. Spoon into stemmed dessert glasses. Serve immediately with spoons and straws.

Only 47 calories per serving.

Fresh Cranberry Frost

Curried Popcorn Mix

Makes about 2 quarts

6 cups unseasoned popped corn
2 cups pretzel sticks
1½ cups DIAMOND® Walnut pieces
¼ cup butter or margarine, melted
2 teaspoons curry powder
¼ teaspoon hot pepper sauce
Salt to taste
1½ cups SUN-MAID® Golden Raisins

In large, deep baking or roasting pan, combine popped corn, pretzels and walnuts. In small bowl, mix butter, curry powder and pepper sauce; drizzle over popcorn mixture and toss to coat evenly. Bake in 300°F oven about 30 minutes, tossing twice. Remove from oven. Mix in salt. Cool completely. Store in airtight container. Mix in raisins before serving.

Teriyaki Scallop Roll-Ups

Makes about 2 dozen appetizers

12 slices bacon, partially cooked and cut in half crosswise
⅓ cup REALIME® Lime Juice from Concentrate
¼ cup soy sauce
¼ cup vegetable oil
1 tablespoon light brown sugar
2 cloves garlic, finely chopped
½ teaspoon pepper
½ pound sea scallops, cut in half
24 fresh pea pods
12 water chestnuts, cut in half

To make teriyaki marinade, combine REALIME® brand, soy sauce, oil, sugar, garlic and pepper; mix well. Wrap 1 scallop half, 1 pea pod and 1 water chestnut half in each bacon slice; secure with wooden pick. Place in shallow baking dish; pour marinade over. Cover; refrigerate 4 hours or overnight, turning occasionally. Preheat oven to 450°F. Place roll-ups on rack in aluminum foil-lined shallow baking pan, bake 6 minutes. Turn; continue baking 6 minutes or until bacon is crisp. Serve hot. Refrigerate leftovers.

Mariachi Drumsticks (top), Potato Wraps (bottom)

Mariachi Drumsticks

Makes about 20 drummettes

1 1/4 cups crushed plain tortilla chips
1 package (1.25 ounces) LAWRY'S® Taco
    Seasoning Mix
18 to 20 chicken drummettes
    Salsa

Preheat oven to 350°F. In large plastic bag, combine tortilla chips with taco seasoning mix. Dampen chicken with water and shake off excess. Place a few pieces at a time in plastic bag; shake thoroughly to coat with chips. Arrange chicken in greased shallow baking pan; bake uncovered 30 minutes or until chicken is crispy. Serve with salsa for dipping.

Potato Wraps

Makes 16 appetizers

4 small new potatoes (1 1/2-inch diameter each)
1/2 teaspoon LAWRY'S® Seasoned Salt
1/2 teaspoon LAWRY'S® Seasoned Pepper
1/4 teaspoon crushed bay leaves
8 slices bacon, cut in half crosswise

Preheat oven to 400°F. Wash potatoes and cut into quarters. Sprinkle each with a mixture of seasoned salt, seasoned pepper and bay leaves. Wrap 1 bacon piece around each potato piece. Sprinkle with any remaining seasonings. Place in baking dish and bake uncovered 20 minutes or until bacon is crispy and potatoes are cooked through. Drain on paper towels. Serve, if desired, with sour cream and chives.

Pineapple Raspberry Punch

Pineapple Raspberry Punch

Makes 9 cups

5 cups DOLE® Pineapple Juice
1 quart raspberry cranberry drink
1 pint fresh or frozen raspberries
1 lemon, thinly sliced
Ice

Chill ingredients. Combine in punch bowl.

French Onion Dip

Makes about 2¹/₂ cups

2 cups sour cream
¹/₂ cup HELLMANN'S® or BEST FOODS® Real,
   Light or Cholesterol Free Reduced Calorie
   Mayonnaise
1 package (1.9 ounces) KNORR® French onion
   soup and recipe mix

In medium bowl combine sour cream, mayonnaise
and soup mix. Cover; chill. Serve with fresh
vegetables or potato chips. Garnish as desired.

Spinach Dip

Makes about 3 cups

1 package (10 ounces) frozen chopped spinach,
   thawed and drained
1¹/₂ cups sour cream
1 cup HELLMANN'S® or BEST FOODS® Real,
   Light or Cholesterol Free Reduced Calorie
   Mayonnaise
1 package (1.4 ounces) KNORR® vegetable soup
   and recipe mix
1 can (8 ounces) water chestnuts, drained and
   chopped (optional)
3 green onions, chopped

In medium bowl combine spinach, sour cream,
mayonnaise, soup mix, water chestnuts and green
onions. Cover; chill. Serve with fresh vegetables,
crackers or chips. Garnish as desired.

Cucumber Dill Dip

Makes about 2¹/₂ cups

1 package (8 ounces) light cream cheese,
   softened
1 cup HELLMANN'S® or BEST FOODS® Real,
   Light or Cholesterol Free Reduced Calorie
   Mayonnaise
2 medium cucumbers, peeled, seeded and
   chopped
2 tablespoons sliced green onions
1 tablespoon lemon juice
2 teaspoons snipped fresh dill *or* ¹/₂ teaspoon
   dried dillweed
¹/₂ teaspoon hot pepper sauce

In medium bowl beat cream cheese until smooth.
Stir in mayonnaise, cucumbers, green onions, lemon
juice, dill and hot pepper sauce. Cover; chill. Serve
with fresh vegetables, crackers or chips. Garnish as
desired.

Left to right: French Onion Dip,
Cucumber Dill Dip, Spinach Dip

Tangy Holiday Meatballs (left), Peanut Butter-Cheese Triangles (right)

Tangy Holiday Meatballs

Makes 3 dozen meatballs (12 appetizer servings)

Meatballs
  1 cup **KELLOGG'S® RICE KRISPIES®**
    cereal
  ²/₃ cup nonfat dry milk powder
  ¹/₄ cup finely chopped onion
  2 tablespoons ketchup
  1 egg
  1 teaspoon salt
  ¹/₈ teaspoon pepper
  1 pound lean ground beef

Sauce
  1 can (15 oz.) tomato sauce
  ¹/₂ cup ketchup
  ¹/₄ cup firmly packed brown sugar
  ¹/₄ cup finely chopped onion
  ¹/₄ cup sweet pickle relish
  2 tablespoons Worcestershire sauce
  1 tablespoon vinegar
  ¹/₄ teaspoon pepper

For meatballs, combine KELLOGG'S® RICE KRISPIES® cereal, dry milk, onion, ketchup, egg, salt and pepper. Add beef, mixing only until combined. Using level measuring-tablespoon, portion meat mixture. Roll into balls and place in foil-lined shallow baking pan. Bake in 400°F oven about 12 minutes or until browned.

In 4-quart saucepan, combine sauce ingredients. Simmer over low heat 15 minutes, stirring frequently. Add meatballs to sauce and continue simmering 10 minutes longer. Serve hot.

Per Serving (3 meatballs): 130 Calories

Note: *Tangy Holiday Meatballs may be served as an entree over hot rice.*

Peanut Butter-Cheese Triangles

Makes 24 triangles

  2 tablespoons nonfat dry milk powder
  ¹/₂ cup corn syrup
  ¹/₂ cup crunchy peanut butter
  3 cups **KELLOGG'S® RICE KRISPIES®** cereal
  2 packages (3 oz. each) cream cheese, softened
  2 cups shredded cheddar cheese
  2 tablespoons margarine or butter, softened

In 2-quart saucepan, combine dry milk and corn syrup, mixing until smooth. Cook over medium heat, stirring constantly, until mixture starts to boil. Remove from heat. Stir in peanut butter. Add KELLOGG'S® RICE KRISPIES® cereal, stirring until cereal is coated. Spread mixture evenly in wax paper-lined 13×9×2-inch pan. Chill until firm.

In food processor or electric mixer bowl, combine cream cheese, cheddar cheese and margarine. Process until cheese is smooth. Cut cereal mixture in half crosswise to form 2 (9×6-inch) rectangles. Set aside ¹/₃ cup cheese mixture and spread remaining cheese on 1 of the cereal rectangles. Place second cereal rectangle on top of cheese, pressing to form a sandwich. Chill until firm, about 2 hours.

To serve, cut cereal into 2-inch squares. Cut squares diagonally into 2 pieces to form triangles. Garnish each triangle with remaining cheese and small parsley leaf. Serve cold.

Per Serving (2 triangles): 270 Calories

Fireside Punch

Makes about 5 servings

1½ cups cranberry juice cocktail
1½ cups cold water
4 bags LIPTON® Cinnamon Apple or Gentle
    Orange Herbal Flo-Thru Tea Bags
2 tablespoons brown sugar
    Cinnamon sticks (optional)
    Fresh cranberries (optional)

In medium saucepan, bring cranberry juice and
water to a boil. Add cinnamon apple herbal tea bags;
cover and brew 5 minutes. Remove tea bags; stir in
sugar. Pour into mugs and garnish with cinnamon
sticks and fresh cranberries.

Stuffed Mushrooms

Makes 12 appetizer servings

1 package (6 oz.) STOVE TOP® Chicken Flavor
    Stuffing Mix
24 large mushrooms (about 1½ lbs.)
¼ cup (½ stick) butter or margarine
¼ cup *each* finely chopped red and green pepper
3 tablespoons butter or margarine, melted

Prepare stuffing mix as directed on package,
omitting butter. Remove stems from mushrooms;
chop stems. Melt ¼ cup butter in skillet. Add
mushroom caps; cook and stir until lightly browned.
Arrange in shallow baking dish. Cook and stir
chopped mushroom stems and the peppers in the
skillet until tender; stir into prepared stuffing. Spoon
onto mushroom caps; drizzle with 3 tablespoons
butter. Place under preheated broiler for 5 minutes
to heat through.

Pina Colada Punch

Makes 15 servings

5 cups DOLE® Pineapple Juice
1 can (15 oz.) real cream of coconut
1 liter lemon-lime soda
2 limes
1½ cups light rum, optional
    Ice cubes
    Mint sprigs

Chill all ingredients. Whir 2 cups pineapple juice
with cream of coconut in blender. Combine pureed
mixture with remaining pineapple juice, soda, juice
of 1 lime, rum (if desired) and ice. Garnish with 1
sliced lime and mint.

Hot Mulled Cider

Makes 8 servings

1 quart apple cider
⅔ cup firmly packed DOMINO® Light Brown
    Sugar
2 small sticks cinnamon
8 whole cloves
¼ teaspoon ground nutmeg
¼ teaspoon ground ginger
    Lemon slices

Combine all ingredients except lemon slices in
saucepan. Bring to a boil, stirring constantly. Reduce
heat; simmer 10 minutes. Remove cinnamon sticks
and cloves. Garnish with lemon slices. Serve at once.

Hot Buttered Rum

Makes 4 cups (16 servings)

1 cup granulated sugar
1 cup firmly packed brown sugar
1 cup LAND O LAKES® Sweet Cream Butter
2 cups vanilla ice cream, softened
    Rum or rum extract
    Boiling water
    Nutmeg

In 2-quart saucepan combine granulated sugar,
brown sugar and butter. Cook over low heat, stirring
occasionally, until butter is melted and sugar is
dissolved (6 to 8 minutes). In large mixer bowl
combine cooked mixture with ice cream; beat at
medium speed, scraping bowl often, until smooth
(1 to 2 minutes). Store refrigerated up to 2 weeks.
For each serving, fill mug with ¼ cup mixture, 1
ounce rum or ¼ teaspoon rum extract and ¾ cup
boiling water; sprinkle with nutmeg.

Tip: Mixture can be frozen up to 1 month.

Hot Buttered Rum

Continental Cheese Mold

Continental Cheese Mold

Makes 4 cups

1 package (4-serving size) **JELL-O®** Brand
    Gelatin, Orange or Lemon Flavor
³/4 cup boiling water
1 container (16 ounces) cottage cheese
2 ounces Roquefort or bleu cheese, crumbled
¹/2 cup sour cream
1 teaspoon seasoned salt
1 teaspoon lemon juice
1 teaspoon Worcestershire sauce
2 tablespoons chopped parsley
    Sliced carrots (optional)
    Watercress (optional)
    Assorted crackers and vegetables

Dissolve gelatin in boiling water. Combine cheeses, sour cream, seasoned salt, lemon juice and Worcestershire sauce in large bowl; beat until smooth. (Or, combine in blender and blend until smooth.) Gradually blend in gelatin. Add parsley. Pour into 4-cup mold or bowl. Chill until set, about 3 hours. Unmold. Garnish with carrot slices and watercress, if desired. Serve with assorted crackers and vegetables.

Preparation time: 15 minutes
Chill time: 3 hours

Steamed Stuffed Zucchini Rounds

Makes 6 to 8 appetizer servings

4 zucchini, 6 to 7 inches long, about 1½ inches in diameter
½ cup KIKKOMAN® Teriyaki Sauce
½ pound ground beef
½ cup dry bread crumbs
¼ cup minced green onions and tops

Trim off and discard ends of zucchini; cut crosswise into ¾-inch lengths. Scoop out flesh, leaving about ⅛-inch shell on sides and bottoms; reserve flesh. Place zucchini rounds in large plastic bag; pour in teriyaki sauce. Press air out of bag; tie top securely. Marinate 30 minutes, turning bag over occasionally. Meanwhile, coarsely chop zucchini flesh; reserve ½ cup. Remove zucchini rounds from marinade; reserve ¼ cup marinade. Combine reserved marinade with beef, bread crumbs, green onions and ½ cup reserved zucchini flesh. Fill each round with about 2 teaspoonfuls beef mixture. Place rounds, filled side up, on steamer rack. Set rack in large pot or wok of boiling water. (Do not allow water level to reach zucchini.) Cover and steam 6 minutes, or until zucchini rounds are tender-crisp when pierced with fork. Serve immediately.

Waikiki Appetizers

Makes 6 to 8 appetizer servings

1½ pounds bulk pork sausage
1 can (20 oz.) pineapple chunks in syrup
½ cup brown sugar, packed
¼ cup lemon juice
2 tablespoons cornstarch
2 tablespoons KIKKOMAN® Soy Sauce
½ cup chopped green pepper
½ cup drained maraschino cherries

Shape sausage into ½- to ¾-inch balls. Place in single layer in baking pan. Bake in 400°F oven 25 minutes, or until cooked; drain on paper towels. Meanwhile, drain pineapple; reserve syrup. Add enough water to syrup to measure 1 cup; combine with brown sugar, lemon juice, cornstarch and soy sauce in large saucepan. Cook and stir until sauce boils and thickens. Fold in green pepper, cherries, pineapple chunks and drained cooked sausage. To serve, turn into chafing dish.

Toasted Almond Party Spread

Makes 2⅓ cups

1 8-oz. pkg. PHILADELPHIA BRAND® Cream Cheese, softened
1½ cups (6 ozs.) shredded CASINO® Brand Natural Swiss Cheese
⅓ cup MIRACLE WHIP® Salad Dressing
2 tablespoons chopped green onions
⅛ teaspoon ground nutmeg
⅛ teaspoon pepper
⅓ cup sliced almonds, toasted

Preheat oven to 350°F. Combine all ingredients; mix well. Spread mixture into 9-inch pie plate or quiche dish. Bake for 15 minutes, stirring after 8 minutes. Garnish with additional toasted sliced almonds, if desired. Serve with assorted crackers or toasted bread cut-outs.

Preparation time: 10 minutes
Baking time: 15 minutes

Steamed Stuffed Zucchini Rounds (top),
Waikiki Appetizers (bottom)

Christmas Carol Punch

Makes about 2 quarts

2 medium red apples
2 quarts clear apple cider
8 cinnamon sticks
2 teaspoons whole cloves
½ cup SUN-MAID® Raisins
  Orange slices
  Lemon slices
¼ cup lemon juice

Core apples; slice into ½-inch rings. In Dutch oven, combine cider, cinnamon, cloves, apple rings and raisins. Bring to boil over high heat; reduce heat to low and simmer 5 to 8 minutes or until apples are just tender. Remove cloves; add orange and lemon slices and lemon juice. Pour into punch bowl. Ladle into large mugs, including an apple ring, some raisins and citrus slices in each serving. Serve with spoons.

Holiday Eggnog

Makes 8 servings

½ cup ice water
½ cup brandy
2 envelopes ALBA® Vanilla Shake
6 large ice cubes
2 egg whites
  Nutmeg

Pour water and brandy into blender container; add ALBA® Shake. Cover; process at low speed, adding ice cubes one at a time. Process at highest speed 60 seconds or until ALBA® mixture is thickened and ice cubes are completely processed. Beat egg whites to form soft peaks; fold into ALBA® mixture. Pour into small cups. Dust with nutmeg.

Only 58 calories per serving.

Holiday Eggnog

Double Berry Coco Punch

Makes about 4 quarts

  Ice Ring, optional, or block of ice
2 (10-ounce) packages frozen strawberries in syrup, thawed
1 (15-ounce) can COCO LOPEZ® Cream of Coconut
1 (48-ounce) bottle cranberry juice cocktail, chilled
2 cups light rum, optional
1 (32-ounce) bottle club soda, chilled

Prepare ice ring in advance if desired. In blender container, puree strawberries with cream of coconut until smooth. In large punch bowl, combine strawberry mixture, cranberry juice and rum if desired. Just before serving, add club soda and ice ring or block of ice.

Ice Ring: Fill ring mold with water to within 1 inch of top rim; freeze. Arrange strawberries, cranberries, mint leaves, lime slices or other fruits on top of ice. Gradually pour small amount of cold water over fruits; freeze.

Beef Kushisashi

Makes 10 to 12 appetizer servings

½ cup KIKKOMAN® Soy Sauce
¼ cup chopped green onions and tops
2 tablespoons sugar
1 tablespoon vegetable oil
1½ teaspoons cornstarch
1 clove garlic, pressed
1 teaspoon grated fresh ginger root
2½ pounds boneless beef sirloin steak

Blend soy sauce, green onions, sugar, oil, cornstarch, garlic and ginger in small saucepan. Simmer, stirring constantly, until thickened, about 1 minute; cool. Cover and set aside. Slice beef into ⅛-inch-thick strips about 4 inches long and 1-inch wide. Thread onto bamboo or metal skewers keeping meat as flat as possible; brush both sides of beef with sauce. Place skewers on rack of broiler pan; broil to desired degree of doneness.

Bacon Appetizer Crescents

Preheat oven to 375°F. Beat cream cheese, bacon, parmesan cheese, onion, parsley and milk in small mixing bowl at medium speed with electric mixer until well blended. Separate dough into eight rectangles; firmly press perforations together to seal. Spread each rectangle with 2 rounded measuring tablespoonfuls cream cheese mixture.

Cut each rectangle in half diagonally; repeat with opposite corners. Cut in half crosswise to form six triangles. Roll up triangles, starting at short ends. Place on greased cookie sheet; brush with combined egg and water. Sprinkle with poppy seed, if desired. Bake 12 to 15 minutes or until golden brown. Serve immediately.

Preparation time: 30 minutes
Cooking time: 15 minutes

Fruity Cheese Spread

Makes about 1½ cups

   8 ounces cream cheese, softened
   1 teaspoon grated orange peel
   ¾ teaspoon almond extract
   ½ teaspoon ground ginger
1½ cups **RALSTON®** brand Fruit Muesli with
      Cranberries, crushed to 1 cup
   Apple and pear slices
   Crackers and cookies

In medium bowl combine cream cheese, orange peel, almond extract and ginger; beat until smooth. Place ½ cup cereal in serving dish; spoon cheese mixture on top. Refrigerate 2 to 3 hours. Just before serving, sprinkle remaining ½ cup cereal over cheese spread. Serve with apple and pear slices, crackers and cookies.

Bacon Appetizer Crescents

Makes about 4 dozen appetizers

1 8-oz. pkg. **PHILADELPHIA BRAND®** Cream
   Cheese, softened
8 **OSCAR MAYER®** Bacon Slices, crisply
   cooked, crumbled
⅓ cup (1½ ozs.) **KRAFT®** 100% Grated
   Parmesan Cheese
¼ cup finely chopped onion
2 tablespoons chopped parsley
1 tablespoon milk
2 8-oz. cans refrigerated crescent dinner rolls
1 egg, beaten
1 teaspoon cold water

Festive Brunches

Egg & Asparagus Casserole

Makes about 4 servings

1 package LIPTON® Rice & Sauce–Asparagus
    with Hollandaise Sauce
1 medium red bell pepper, chopped
1/2 cup sliced green onions
8 eggs, beaten
2 cups milk
1 cup water
2 tablespoons butter or margarine, cut into
    small pieces
1 tablespoon Dijon-style mustard
3/4 teaspoon salt
1/4 teaspoon pepper
2 cups shredded Swiss cheese (about 8 ounces)

In large bowl, combine all ingredients except 1/2 cup cheese. Chill at least 6 hours or overnight.

Preheat oven to 350°F. Pour egg mixture into greased 11×7-inch baking pan. Sprinkle with remaining 1/2 cup cheese. Bake 45 minutes or until set.

Skillet Walnut Pumpkin Bread

Makes 6 to 8 servings

  Cornmeal
1/3 cup butter or margarine, softened
1 cup sugar
2 eggs, slightly beaten
1 cup canned pumpkin
3/4 cup milk
1 cup all-purpose flour
3/4 cup cornmeal
1 teaspoon ground allspice
1 teaspoon baking soda
1/2 teaspoon baking powder
1 cup chopped DIAMOND® Walnuts
  DIAMOND® Walnut halves, for garnish

Grease 9-inch cast-iron skillet. Dust with cornmeal; set aside. In large bowl, beat butter, sugar and eggs. Add pumpkin and milk; mix to blend thoroughly. In medium bowl, combine flour, the 3/4 cup cornmeal, allspice, baking soda and baking powder. Add to wet ingredients, stirring just until blended. Stir in chopped walnuts. Pour into prepared skillet. Garnish center with walnut halves. Bake in preheated 375°F oven 45 minutes or until pick inserted into center comes out clean. Serve warm.

Note: Substitute a deep 9-inch round or square baking pan if cast-iron skillet is unavailable.

Spinach Cheese Torta

Makes about 8 servings

3 medium corn muffins, crumbled (about
   2¹/₂ cups crumbs)
3 tablespoons butter or margarine, melted
3 teaspoons chopped fresh basil leaves*
   Salt and pepper to taste
1 tablespoon olive or vegetable oil
2 teaspoons finely chopped garlic
1 package (10 ounces) frozen chopped spinach,
   thawed and squeezed dry
1 cup ricotta cheese
¹/₄ cup grated Parmesan cheese
1 egg, slightly beaten
1 package LIPTON® Rice & Sauce–Cheddar
   Broccoli
1¹/₂ cups shredded mozzarella cheese (about
   6 ounces)

Preheat oven to 400°F. In medium bowl, thoroughly combine corn muffin crumbs, butter, 2 teaspoons basil, salt and pepper. Press into bottom and ¹/₂ inch up sides of 9-inch springform or square baking pan. Bake 12 minutes; cool on wire rack.

In medium saucepan, heat oil and cook garlic over medium heat 30 seconds. Add spinach and cook over medium heat, stirring constantly, 2 minutes or until heated through; add salt and pepper. Stir in ricotta cheese, Parmesan cheese, egg and remaining 1 teaspoon basil; set aside.

Prepare rice & Cheddar broccoli sauce according to package directions. Into prepared pan, layer ³/₄ cup mozzarella cheese, rice mixture, spinach mixture, then remaining ³/₄ cup mozzarella cheese. Decrease heat to 375°F and bake 30 minutes or until set. Remove sides of springform pan. Garnish as desired. Serve warm or cool.

*Substitution: Use ¹/₂ teaspoon dried basil leaves in crust and 1 teaspoon dried basil leaves in filling.

Spinach Cheese Torta

Noel Bran Muffins

Makes 12 muffins

1¹/₄ cups whole bran cereal
1 cup milk
1¹/₂ cups flour
 ¹/₂ cup firmly packed brown sugar
 ¹/₂ cup shredded carrots
2 teaspoons baking powder
¹/₄ teaspoon salt
¹/₄ teaspoon nutmeg
¹/₄ cup butter or margarine, melted
2 eggs
1 cup chopped DEL MONTE®
   Dried Apricots or Seedless Raisins

Soften bran in milk. In large bowl, blend together flour, sugar, carrots, baking powder, salt and nutmeg. Combine bran mixture, butter and eggs; add to dry ingredients. Stir until flour is moistened. Fold in chopped apricots or raisins. Fill 12 paper-lined or greased 2¹/₂-inch muffin-pan cups. Bake at 375°F, 25 to 30 minutes or until golden. Serve warm.

Crab & Shrimp Quiche

Makes one 9-inch quiche

1 (9-inch) unbaked pastry shell
6 slices BORDEN® Process American Cheese
   Food
2 tablespoons sliced green onion
2 tablespoons chopped pimiento
1 tablespoon flour
1 (6-ounce) can ORLEANS® or HARRIS®
   Crabmeat, drained
1 (4¹/₄-ounce) can ORLEANS® Shrimp, drained
   and soaked as label directs
1¹/₂ cups BORDEN® or MEADOW GOLD®
   Half-and-Half
3 eggs, beaten

Place rack in lowest position in oven; preheat oven to 425°F. Cut *4 slices* cheese food into pieces. In large bowl, toss cheese food pieces, onion and pimiento with flour. Add remaining ingredients except pastry shell and cheese food slices. Pour into pastry shell. Bake 20 minutes. Reduce oven temperature to 325°F; bake 20 minutes longer or until set. Arrange remaining *2 slices* cheese food on top of quiche. Let stand 10 minutes before serving. Garnish as desired. Refrigerate leftovers.

Quiche Florentine

Makes 6 to 8 servings

1 15-oz. pkg. refrigerated pie crusts
2 cups (8 ozs.) VELVEETA® Shredded
    Pasteurized Process Cheese Food
1/3 cup (1 1/2 ozs.) KRAFT® 100% Grated
    Parmesan Cheese
1 10-oz. pkg. frozen chopped spinach, thawed,
    well drained
4 crisply cooked bacon slices, crumbled
3/4 cup milk
3 eggs, beaten
1/4 teaspoon pepper

Prepare pie crust according to package directions for filled one-crust pie using 9-inch pie plate. (Refrigerate remaining crust for later use.) In large bowl, combine remaining ingredients; mix well. Pour into unbaked pie crust. Bake at 350°F, 35 to 40 minutes or until knife inserted in center comes out clean. Let stand 10 minutes before serving.

Preparation time: 15 minutes
Baking time: 40 minutes plus standing

Nutcracker Fruit Bread

Makes 6 mini loaves

2 1/4 cups all-purpose flour
1 1/2 cups sugar
1 cup LAND O LAKES® Sweet Cream Butter,
    softened
1 (8-oz.) pkg. cream cheese, softened
4 eggs
1 1/2 teaspoons baking powder
1 1/2 teaspoons vanilla
1 cup candied red and green cherries, quartered
1/2 cup chopped dates
1/2 cup golden raisins
1/2 cup chopped walnuts

Heat oven to 325°F. In large mixer bowl combine 1 1/4 cups flour, the sugar, butter, cream cheese, eggs, baking powder and vanilla. Beat at medium speed, scraping bowl often, until well mixed (2 to 3 minutes). By hand, stir in remaining 1 cup flour, candied cherries, dates, raisins and walnuts. Pour into 6 greased 5 1/2×3-inch mini-loaf pans. Bake for 45 to 55 minutes or until wooden pick inserted in center comes out clean. Cool 10 minutes; remove from pans. Cool completely.

Puffy Tuna Omelet

Puffy Tuna Omelet

Makes 1 serving

2 eggs, separated
1/4 teaspoon pepper
1 tablespoon water
1 tablespoon butter or margarine
2 tablespoons chicken broth
1/2 small red or green bell pepper, cut into strips
1 cup chopped spinach leaves
1 can (3 1/4 ounces) STARKIST® Tuna, drained
    and broken into chunks
1/4 teaspoon dried oregano, crushed
    Salt and pepper to taste
2 teaspoons grated Parmesan cheese

In a small bowl beat egg yolks and pepper on high speed of electric mixer about 5 minutes, or until thick and lemon-colored. In a medium bowl beat egg whites and water until stiff peaks form. Pour yolks over whites and gently fold in.

Preheat oven to 325°F. In a 7-inch nonstick skillet with ovenproof handle melt butter over low heat. Lift and tilt skillet to coat sides. Pour egg mixture into hot skillet, mounding it slightly higher around edges. Cook over low heat about 6 minutes, or until eggs are puffed and set and bottom is golden brown. Bake for 6 to 8 minutes, or until a knife inserted near center comes out clean.

Meanwhile, in a small skillet heat chicken broth. Cook and stir bell pepper and spinach in broth for 2 minutes. Stir in tuna and oregano; season to taste with salt and pepper. Drain; keep warm. Loosen sides of omelet with spatula. Make a shallow cut across omelet, cutting slightly off center; fill with tuna mixture. Fold smaller portion of omelet over larger portion. Sprinkle with cheese. Serve immediately.

Preparation time: 10 minutes

Calorie count: 422 calories per serving.

Caramel Pecan Sticky Buns

Caramel Pecan Sticky Buns

Makes 2 dozen

1 8-oz. pkg. PHILADELPHIA BRAND® Cream
  Cheese, cubed
3/4 cup cold water
1 16-oz. pkg. hot roll mix
1 egg
1/3 cup granulated sugar
1 teaspoon cinnamon
1 cup pecan halves
3/4 cup packed brown sugar
1/2 cup light corn syrup
1/4 cup PARKAY® Margarine, melted

Preheat oven to 350°F. Stir together 6 ounces cream cheese and water in small saucepan. Cook over low heat until mixture reaches 115° to 120°F, stirring occasionally. Stir together hot roll mix and yeast packet in large bowl. Add cream cheese mixture and egg, mixing until dough pulls away from sides of bowl. Knead dough on lightly floured surface 5 minutes or until smooth and elastic. Cover; let rise in warm place 20 minutes.

Beat remaining cream cheese, granulated sugar and cinnamon in small mixing bowl at medium speed with electric mixer until well blended. Roll out dough to 18×12-inch rectangle; spread cream cheese mixture over dough to within 1 inch from outer edges of dough. Roll up from long end; seal edges. Cut into twenty-four 3/4-inch slices.

Stir together remaining ingredients in small bowl. Spoon 2 teaspoonfuls mixture into bottoms of greased medium-sized muffin pans. Place dough, cut side up, in cups. Cover; let rise in warm place 30 minutes. Bake 20 to 25 minutes or until golden brown. Invert onto serving platter immediately.

Preparation time: 30 minutes plus rising
Cooking time: 25 minutes

Cream Cheese and Pecan Danish

Makes 10 to 12 servings

1 sheet frozen puff pastry, thawed
2 3-oz. pkgs. PHILADELPHIA BRAND®
  Cream Cheese, softened
1/4 cup powdered sugar
1 egg
1 teaspoon vanilla
3/4 cup chopped pecans
  Creamy Glaze

Preheat oven to 375°F. Unfold pastry; roll to 15×10-inch rectangle. Place in 15×10×1-inch jelly roll pan. Beat 6 ounces cream cheese, 1/4 cup sugar, egg and vanilla in small mixing bowl at medium speed with electric mixer until well blended. Stir in 1/2 cup pecans. Spread cream cheese mixture over pastry to within 3 inches from outer edges. Make 2-inch cuts at 1-inch intervals on long sides of pastry. Crisscross strips over filling. Bake 25 to 30 minutes or until golden brown. Cool. Drizzle with Creamy Glaze. Sprinkle with remaining pecans.

Creamy Glaze

1 3-oz. pkg. PHILADELPHIA BRAND® Cream
  Cheese, softened
3/4 cup powdered sugar
1 tablespoon milk

Beat ingredients until smooth.

Preparation time: 20 minutes
Cooking time: 30 minutes

Cranberry Conserve

Makes 3 1/2 cups

1 (12-ounce) package fresh cranberries
1 1/2 large seedless oranges, cut into wedges
1 1/2 cups DOMINO® Granulated Sugar
1/3 cup cherry brandy

Place all ingredients into blender or food processor container; blend until coarsely chopped. Store, covered, in refrigerator.

Cream Cheese and Pecan Danish

Welsh Rarebit

Welsh Rarebit

Makes 4 servings

¹/₂ cup **HELLMANN'S®** or **BEST FOODS®** Real,
    Light or Cholesterol Free Reduced Calorie
    Mayonnaise
 3 tablespoons flour
¹/₂ teaspoon dry mustard
¹/₂ teaspoon Worcestershire sauce
³/₄ cup beer
 2 cups (8 ounces) shredded Cheddar cheese
 8 slices white or whole wheat bread, toasted,
    halved diagonally
 3 large tomatoes, cut into 16 slices

In 2-quart saucepan combine mayonnaise, flour, dry
mustard and Worcestershire sauce. Stirring
constantly, cook over low heat 1 minute. Gradually
stir in beer until thick and smooth (do not boil). Stir
in cheese until melted. Arrange 4 toast halves and 4
tomato slices alternately on each of 4 serving plates;
spoon on cheese sauce. Serve immediately.

Microwave Directions: In 2-quart microwavable bowl
combine mayonnaise, flour, dry mustard and
Worcestershire sauce. Gradually stir in beer and
cheese. Microwave on HIGH (100%), 4 minutes,
stirring vigorously after each minute. Serve as above.

Easy Spinach Soufflé

Makes 4 to 6 servings

¹/₂ cup **HELLMANN'S®** or **BEST FOODS®** Real,
    Light or Cholesterol Free Reduced Calorie
    Mayonnaise
¹/₄ cup flour
 2 tablespoons grated onion
³/₄ teaspoon salt
¹/₄ teaspoon nutmeg
¹/₄ teaspoon freshly ground pepper
 1 cup milk
 1 package (10 ounces) frozen chopped spinach,
    thawed and well drained on paper towels
 4 eggs, separated
¹/₄ teaspoon cream of tartar

Preheat oven to 400°F. Grease 2-quart soufflé dish.
In 3-quart saucepan combine mayonnaise, flour,
onion, salt, nutmeg and pepper. Stirring constantly,
cook over medium heat 1 minute. Gradually stir in
milk until smooth. Stirring constantly, cook until
thick. Remove from heat. Stir in spinach. Beat in
egg yolks. In small bowl with mixer at high speed,
beat egg whites with cream of tartar until stiff peaks
form. Gently fold into spinach mixture. Spoon into
prepared dish. Place on lowest rack of oven.
Immediately reduce oven temperature to 375°F. Bake
40 minutes or until top is puffed and golden brown.
Serve immediately.

Chocolate Spice Surprise Muffins

Makes about 1¹/₂ dozen

¹/₃ cup firmly packed light brown sugar
¹/₄ cup margarine or butter, softened
 1 egg
 1 cup **BORDEN®** or **MEADOW GOLD®** Milk
 2 cups biscuit baking mix
¹/₃ cup unsweetened cocoa
 1 (9-ounce) package **NONE SUCH®** Condensed
    Mincemeat, crumbled
18 solid milk chocolate candy drops
¹/₂ cup confectioners' sugar
 1 tablespoon water

Preheat oven to 375°F. In large mixer bowl, beat
brown sugar and margarine until fluffy. Add egg and
milk; mix well. Stir in biscuit mix, cocoa and
mincemeat until moistened. Fill greased or paper-
lined muffin cups ³/₄ full. Top with candy drop; press
into batter. Bake 15 to 20 minutes. Cool 5 minutes;
remove from pan. Meanwhile, mix confectioners'
sugar and water; drizzle over warm muffins.

Fruited Pain Perdu

Makes 6 to 8 servings

4 eggs, slightly beaten
1¼ cups milk
1 teaspoon vanilla extract
½ teaspoon ground cinnamon
⅛ teaspoon salt
1 large loaf Italian bread, cut diagonally into
  1-inch slices
2 to 3 tablespoons butter or margarine
1 cup shredded GJETOST® cheese
Mixed Fruit Sauce (recipe follows)

In large, shallow baking dish, blend eggs, milk,
vanilla, cinnamon and salt. Add bread, turning to
moisten on both sides. Cover; refrigerate overnight.

In large skillet, melt 1 tablespoon butter. Add several
slices of bread. Cook over low heat until browned.
Turn slices; top with some of the cheese. Brown on
second side. Repeat with remaining bread and
cheese, adding additional butter to skillet as
necessary. Serve with Mixed Fruit Sauce.

Mixed Fruit Sauce

1 can (16 ounces) pineapple chunks
1 cup orange juice
2 tablespoons lemon juice
2 teaspoons cornstarch
1 large banana, sliced
1 cup diced papaya
1 teaspoon grated orange peel

Drain pineapple, reserving juice. In large saucepan,
combine pineapple juice, orange and lemon juices
and cornstarch. Stir to dissolve cornstarch. Cook
over medium heat, stirring until thickened and
smooth. Add fruits and orange peel. Makes about
2½ cups.

Jeweled Coffee Cake

Makes 1 coffee cake

Coffee Cake
8 ounces cream cheese, softened
2 tablespoons granulated sugar
1 teaspoon ground cinnamon
1 cup grated apple
1 loaf frozen bread dough, thawed
2 cups RALSTON® brand Fruit Muesli with
  Cranberries

Glaze
¾ cup powdered sugar
4 teaspoons cranberry juice or milk

To prepare Coffee Cake: Lightly grease baking sheet.
In medium bowl combine cream cheese, granulated
sugar and cinnamon; stir in apple. Set aside. On
floured surface roll dough into 18×9-inch rectangle.
Spread cream cheese mixture evenly over dough.
Sprinkle cereal over cheese mixture. Starting with
long side, roll dough into cylinder. Place on prepared
baking sheet seam side down; bring ends together to
form circle. Pinch ends together to seal. Cut slits
halfway through dough 1½ inches apart around
entire circle. Cover with towel; let rise in warm place
1 hour or until doubled in size. Preheat oven to
350°F. Bake, uncovered, 20 to 22 minutes or until
golden brown. Cool on wire rack 5 minutes; drizzle
glaze over coffee cake.

To prepare Glaze: In small bowl beat powdered sugar
with cranberry juice until smooth.

Jeweled Coffee Cake

Moist Orange Mince Muffins

Makes about 1½ dozen

2 cups unsifted flour
½ cup sugar
1 tablespoon baking powder
1 teaspoon salt
½ teaspoon baking soda
1 egg, slightly beaten
1 (8-ounce) container BORDEN® LITE-LINE®
    or VIVA® Orange Yogurt
⅓ cup BORDEN® or MEADOW GOLD® Milk
⅓ cup vegetable oil
1 (9-ounce) package NONE SUCH® Condensed
    Mincemeat, finely crumbled
⅓ cup BAMA® Orange Marmalade, melted,
    optional

Preheat oven to 400°F. In large bowl, combine dry ingredients. In medium bowl, combine egg, yogurt, milk, oil and mincemeat; mix well. Stir into flour mixture only until moistened. Fill greased or paper-lined muffin cups ¾ full. Bake 20 to 25 minutes or until golden. Immediately remove from pans. Brush warm muffins with marmalade if desired. Serve warm.

Moist Orange Mince Muffins

Cinnamon Apple Coffee Cake

Makes about 8 servings

1½ cups boiling water
5 LIPTON® Cinnamon Apple Herbal Tea Bags
½ cup confectioners sugar
1 cup all-purpose flour
½ cup sugar
6 tablespoons IMPERIAL® Margarine, melted
1 egg
1 teaspoon baking powder
¼ teaspoon salt
¼ cup golden raisins
1 cup chopped apples
½ cup chopped walnuts
½ teaspoon grated lemon peel

Preheat oven to 375°F. In teapot, pour boiling water over cinnamon apple herbal tea bags. Cover and brew 5 minutes. Remove tea bags. In 1-quart saucepan, combine ¾ cup tea with confectioners sugar. Chill remaining tea at least 10 minutes. Boil tea-sugar mixture over medium-high heat 7 minutes or until thick and syrupy.

In large bowl, combine chilled tea, flour, sugar, margarine, egg, baking powder and salt. With electric mixer or rotary beater, beat to moisten, then beat at medium speed 2 minutes. Fold in raisins and ½ cup apples. Spread into greased 8-inch round cake pan. Bake 25 minutes or until toothpick inserted in center comes out clean. On wire rack, cool 10 minutes. Garnish, if desired, with apple slices.

In small bowl, combine tea-sugar glaze with remaining ½ cup apples, walnuts and lemon peel. Spoon over warm cake and serve.

Apple-Cranberry Relish

Makes about 4½ cups

2 unpeeled oranges, quartered and seeded
2 unpeeled Empire apples, quartered and cored
1 pound fresh cranberries
1 cup sugar (or to taste)

Chop oranges, apples and cranberries in food processor into fine pieces. Add sugar and mix well. Store, covered, in refrigerator. This relish gets better as it seasons.

Favorite recipe from **Western New York Apple Growers Association, Inc.**

Layered Vegetable Pie

Layered Vegetable Pie

Makes 6 main-course or 12 appetizer servings

2 tablespoons vegetable or olive oil
1 package (16 ounces) **CAMPBELL'S FRESH®** mushrooms, sliced
¼ cup finely chopped shallots or onion
1 medium clove garlic, minced
1 package (10 ounces) frozen chopped spinach, cooked and well drained
1 tablespoon all-purpose flour
4 eggs, slightly beaten
1 container (15 ounces) ricotta cheese
¼ cup grated Parmesan cheese
¾ cup diced fontinella or mozzarella cheese
¼ teaspoon ground nutmeg
¼ teaspoon pepper
Pastry for 2-crust 10-inch pie
1 egg, separated
1 jar (6 ounces) roasted red peppers, drained and cut into strips
1 tablespoon sour cream or heavy cream

In 10-inch skillet over medium heat, in hot oil, cook mushrooms and shallots with garlic until tender, stirring occasionally. Add spinach; cook 2 minutes or until liquid is evaporated, stirring constantly. Stir in flour; set aside.

Preheat oven to 375°F. In large bowl, beat together 4 eggs, cheeses, nutmeg and pepper. Stir 1 cup of the cheese mixture into mushroom mixture.

On lightly floured surface, roll half of the pastry into 13-inch round. Line 10-inch deep-dish pie plate with pastry; trim even with rim, saving scraps. Prick with a fork. Brush with beaten egg white. Bake 10 minutes.

In prebaked piecrust, layer: 2 cups of the mushroom mixture, 1 cup of the cheese mixture, remaining mushroom mixture, red peppers and remaining cheese mixture. Roll remaining pastry to 12-inch round. Cut slits. Place over filling; trim edge to ½ inch beyond rim of pie plate. Fold top crust under, forming a ridge. Flute edge. Reroll any pastry scraps and use to decorate top of pastry. In cup, combine egg yolk and sour cream; brush on pastry. Place pie plate on cookie sheet. Bake 1 hour or until golden brown. Let cool on wire rack 20 minutes. Cut into wedges.

Maple French Toast

Makes 4 to 6 servings

¼ cup **CARY'S®, VERMONT MAPLE
    ORCHARDS** or **MACDONALD'S** Pure
    Maple Syrup
¼ cup **BORDEN®** or **MEADOW GOLD®** Milk
 2 eggs, beaten
12 (¾-inch) slices French or Italian bread
    Butter

In medium bowl, combine all ingredients except
bread and butter. Dip bread into egg mixture. In
large greased skillet, cook bread in butter until
golden. Serve warm with Maple Butter and pure
maple syrup.

Maple Butter: In small mixer bowl, beat ½ cup
softened unsalted butter and 2 tablespoons pure
maple syrup until light and fluffy. Makes about
⅔ cup.

Maple French Toast with Maple Butter

Sweet & Spicy Nuts

Makes 3½ cups

¼ cup **LAND O LAKES®** Sweet Cream Butter
 2 cups (8 oz.) pecan halves
½ cup (2 oz.) blanched whole almonds
½ cup (2 oz.) filberts
½ cup plus 3 tablespoons sugar
 2 teaspoons cumin
1½ teaspoons salt

In 10-inch skillet melt butter over medium heat. Stir
in nuts and ½ cup sugar; continue cooking, stirring
constantly, until sugar is melted and nuts are brown
(10 to 12 minutes). Meanwhile, in large bowl stir
together 3 tablespoons sugar, cumin and salt. Stir in
caramelized nuts. Spread onto waxed paper; cool.
Break clusters into individual nuts.

Banana Spice Coffee Cake

Makes one 10-inch coffee cake

2 extra-ripe medium **DOLE®** Bananas, peeled
    and cut into chunks
1/2 cup packed brown sugar
1 teaspoon ground cinnamon
1/4 teaspoon ground nutmeg
1/2 cup margarine
3/4 cup chopped walnuts
1 cup all-purpose flour
1 cup whole wheat flour
1 teaspoon baking powder
1 teaspoon baking soda
1/2 teaspoon salt
1/2 cup granulated sugar
3 eggs
1 teaspoon vanilla
1 cup **DOLE®** Raisins

In food processor or blender, puree bananas (1 cup puree). In small bowl, combine brown sugar, cinnamon and nutmeg. Cut in 1/4 cup of the margarine until mixture resembles coarse crumbs. Stir in walnuts; set aside. In small bowl, combine flours, baking powder, baking soda and salt. In large bowl, beat remaining 1/4 cup margarine and the granulated sugar until light and fluffy. Beat in eggs and vanilla. Add flour mixture to egg mixture alternately with bananas, ending with flour mixture and beating well after each addition. Stir in raisins. Spread half the batter in greased and floured 10-inch tube pan. Sprinkle with half the brown sugar mixture. Repeat layers. Bake in preheated 350°F oven 45 to 50 minutes or until wooden pick inserted into center of cake comes out clean. Let cool in pan on wire rack 10 minutes. Loosen edge; remove from pan. Cool completely on wire rack.

Merry Cranberry Bread

Merry Cranberry Bread

Makes 1 loaf

3/4 cup **MIRACLE WHIP®** Salad Dressing
2 cups flour
1 12-oz. pkg. (1 1/4 cups) cranberry orange sauce
3/4 cup sugar
1/2 cup chopped walnuts
2 eggs, beaten
1 teaspoon baking soda
1/2 teaspoon salt

Mix together all ingredients. Pour into greased 9×5-inch loaf pan. Bake at 350°F, 45 to 50 minutes or until edges pull away from sides of pan. Let stand 10 minutes; remove from pan.

Preparation time: 5 minutes
Cooking time: 50 minutes

Turkey and Caper Quiche

Makes 4 servings

¾ cup diced cooked **BUTTERBALL®** turkey
  Pastry for single 9-inch pie crust*
½ cup (2 ounces) shredded Swiss cheese
⅓ cup diced tomato
¼ cup minced onion
1 tablespoon capers, drained
3 eggs, beaten
1 teaspoon Dijon mustard
1 teaspoon seasoned salt
1 cup half and half

Preheat oven to 350°F. Line 9-inch quiche dish or pie pan with pastry. Trim edge and flute. Layer turkey, cheese, tomato, onion and capers in crust. Blend eggs, mustard, salt and half and half in small bowl. Pour mixture into pie crust. Bake 40 to 50 minutes or until knife inserted 1 inch from center comes out clean.

Substitute frozen 9-inch deep dish pie crust, thawed, for pastry. Omit quiche dish; bake directly in foil pan.

Orange Marmalade Bread

Makes 1 loaf

3 cups all-purpose flour
4 teaspoons baking powder
1 teaspoon salt
½ cup chopped walnuts
2 eggs, lightly beaten
¾ cup **SMUCKER'S®** Simply Fruit Orange
  Marmalade
¾ cup milk
¼ cup honey
2 tablespoons vegetable oil

Preheat oven to 350°F. Grease 9×5×3-inch loaf pan. Into a large bowl, sift together flour, baking powder and salt. Stir in nuts. In small bowl, combine eggs, marmalade, milk, honey and oil; blend well. Add to flour mixture; stir only until flour is well moistened (batter will be lumpy). Turn batter into prepared pan. Bake 65 to 70 minutes or until lightly browned and a wooden toothpick inserted into center comes out clean. Cool in pan on rack 10 minutes. Remove from pan; cool completely on rack.

Turkey and Caper Quiche

Crab and Artichoke Crepe Towers

Makes 8 main-dish or 16 appetizer servings

20 ALMOND DELIGHT® Crepes (recipe follows)
  2 tablespoons margarine or butter
  1 cup sliced mushrooms
  ¼ cup chopped onion
  3 tablespoons all-purpose flour
2½ cups milk
  ½ cup grated Parmesan cheese
  1 package (9 oz.) frozen artichoke hearts,
     prepared according to package directions,
     coarsely chopped
  8 ounces frozen or canned crab, drained
  2 tablespoons chopped fresh parsley
    Salt and pepper to taste

Prepare crepes; set aside. In large saucepan over medium heat, melt margarine. Add mushrooms and onion; cook, stirring constantly, until onion is transparent. Stir in flour. Gradually add milk, stirring until sauce is smooth and has slightly thickened. Stir in cheese, artichokes, crab and parsley; add salt and pepper. Place 1 crepe on serving plate. Spread 2 tablespoons crab and artichoke filling on top. Repeat layers to form a stack with 10 layers, ending with filling. Use remaining crepes and filling to form a second stack. Cut into wedges to serve.

Almond Delight® Crepes

  3 cups ALMOND DELIGHT® brand cereal,
     crushed to 1½ cups
1¼ cups all-purpose flour
  3 eggs
  2 cups milk
  3 tablespoons margarine or butter, melted

In large bowl combine cereal, flour and eggs; gradually add milk and margarine, beating until smooth. Cover; refrigerate several hours or overnight to thicken. (Batter should be consistency of heavy cream. If too thick, add 2 to 3 tablespoons milk. If too thin, add 2 to 3 tablespoons flour.) Cook on crepe maker following manufacturer's instructions. Or, lightly grease 5- to 6-inch skillet. Heat skillet over medium heat; remove from heat. Pour 2 tablespoons batter into pan; tilt pan until batter is spread evenly over bottom. Return to heat, cooking until surface looks dry and bottom of crepe is slightly brown. Invert pan allowing crepe to fall onto plate. Repeat with remaining batter. To make ahead of time, stack crepes with waxed paper between, place in plastic bag and freeze. Let crepes thaw at room temperature 1 hour before using. Makes 22 to 24 crepes.

Crab and Artichoke Crepe Towers

Cranberry All-Bran® Muffins

Makes 12 muffins

1¼ cups all-purpose flour
  ½ cup sugar
  ¼ teaspoon salt
  1 tablespoon baking powder
  ½ teaspoon pumpkin pie spice
1½ cups KELLOGG'S® ALL-BRAN® cereal
1¼ cups skim milk
  2 egg whites
  ¼ cup vegetable oil
  1 cup coarsely chopped cranberries
  ½ cup raisins
  1 teaspoon grated orange peel

Stir together flour, sugar, salt, baking powder and pumpkin pie spice; set aside. Measure KELLOGG'S® ALL-BRAN® cereal and milk into large mixing bowl; stir to combine. Let stand 2 minutes or until cereal is softened. Add egg whites and oil; beat well. Stir in cranberries, raisins and orange peel. Add dry ingredients to cereal mixture, stirring only until combined. Divide batter evenly among 12 greased 2½-inch muffin-pan cups. Bake in 400°F oven about 22 minutes or until lightly browned; serve hot.

Per Serving (1 muffin): 180 calories, 5g dietary fiber, 6g fat

Salads & Side Dishes

Spiced Cranberry-Orange Mold

Makes 10 servings

1 bag (12 ounces) fresh cranberries*
1/2 cup sugar*
2 packages (4-serving size each) *or* 1 package (8-serving size) JELL-O® Brand Gelatin, Orange or Lemon Flavor
1 1/2 cups boiling water
1 cup cold water*
1 tablespoon lemon juice
1/4 teaspoon ground cinnamon
1/8 teaspoon ground cloves
1 orange, sectioned and diced
1/2 cup chopped walnuts
Orange slices (optional)
White kale or curly leaf lettuce (optional)

Chop cranberries finely in food processor. Mix with sugar; set aside. Dissolve gelatin in boiling water. Add cold water, lemon juice, cinnamon and cloves. Chill until thickened. Fold in cranberries, orange and nuts. Spoon into 5-cup mold. Chill until firm, about 4 hours. Unmold. Garnish with orange slices and kale, if desired.

Preparation time: 20 minutes
Chill time: 4 hours

You may substitute 1 can (16 ounces) whole berry cranberry sauce for fresh cranberries. Omit sugar and reduce cold water to 1/2 cup.

Crowd-Pleasing Vegetable Pilaf

Makes 8 to 10 servings

3 cups cooked unsalted regular rice (1 cup uncooked)
1 can (10 3/4 ounces) condensed cream of mushroom soup
1 can (10 3/4 ounces) condensed cream of celery soup
1 cup (4 ounces) shredded Cheddar cheese
1 jar (2 ounces) diced pimiento, drained
1 package (10 ounces) frozen chopped spinach, thawed and well drained
1 package (10 ounces) frozen chopped broccoli, thawed and drained
1 can (2.8 ounces) DURKEE® French Fried Onions

Preheat oven to 350°F. To hot rice in saucepan, add soups, cheese and pimiento; stir well and set aside. In medium bowl, combine spinach, broccoli and 1/2 *can* French Fried Onions. Spread *half* the rice mixture in 12×8-inch baking dish; top with vegetable mixture, then with remaining rice mixture. Bake, covered, for 40 minutes or until heated through. Top with remaining onions; bake, uncovered, 5 minutes or until onions are golden brown.

Microwave Directions: Prepare rice and vegetable mixtures and layer as above in 12×8-inch microwave-safe dish. Cook, covered, on HIGH 12 to 14 minutes or until heated through. Rotate dish halfway through cooking time. Top with remaining onions; cook, uncovered, 1 minute. Let stand 5 minutes.

Spiced Cranberry-Orange Mold

Raisin Almond Stuffing

Makes 3³/4 cups

1 package (6 oz.) **STOVE TOP®** Stuffing Mix,
 any variety
1²/3 cups water*
¹/2 cup raisins
¹/4 cup (¹/2 stick) butter or margarine
¹/2 cup (2 oz.) slivered almonds

Combine contents of vegetable/seasoning packet,
water and raisins in medium saucepan. Add butter.
Bring to a boil. Reduce heat; cover and simmer 5
minutes. Add stuffing crumbs and almonds; stir to
moisten. Cover; remove from heat and let stand 5
minutes. Fluff with fork.

**For moister stuffing, increase water by 2 tablespoons; for less
moist stuffing, decrease water by 2 tablespoons.*

Cheesy Broccoli 'n Mushroom Bake

Makes 6 to 8 servings

2 10-oz. pkgs. frozen broccoli spears, thawed
1 10³/4-oz. can condensed cream of mushroom
 soup
¹/2 cup **MIRACLE WHIP®** Salad Dressing
¹/2 cup milk
1 cup (4 ozs.) 100% Natural **KRAFT®** Shredded
 Cheddar Cheese
¹/2 cup coarsely crushed croutons

Preheat oven to 350°F. Arrange broccoli in 12×8-inch
baking dish. Whisk together soup, salad dressing and
milk. Pour over broccoli. Sprinkle with cheese and
croutons. Bake 30 to 35 minutes or until heated
through.

Preparation time: 10 minutes
Baking time: 30 to 35 minutes

Cheesy Broccoli 'n Mushroom Bake

Confetti Chicken Salad

Makes 6 servings

¹/4 cup white vinegar
3 tablespoons Chef Paul Prudhomme's
 POULTRY MAGIC®
1 teaspoon ground allspice
¹/2 teaspoon ground bay leaf
¹/2 teaspoon salt
1 cup vegetable oil
4 cups cooked rice
12 ounces cooked chicken, cut into bite-size
 pieces
2 cups small broccoli florets
2 cups chopped fresh tomatoes
1 cup shredded carrots
¹/2 cup chopped onion
¹/2 cup chopped celery
 Lettuce leaves

Make dressing by combining vinegar, POULTRY
MAGIC®, allspice, bay leaf and salt in food
processor. Process until well mixed. With motor
running, add oil in slow steady stream until
incorporated and dressing is thick and creamy.
Combine remaining measured ingredients in a large
mixing bowl. Mix well. Stir in dressing. To serve,
line 6 serving plates with lettuce leaves. Divide salad
into portions. Mound each portion of salad onto
center of lettuce leaf.

Turkey Waldorf Salad

Makes about 4 to 6 servings

²/3 cup **HELLMANN'S®** or **BEST FOODS®** Real,
 Light or Cholesterol Free Reduced Calorie
 Mayonnaise
2 tablespoons lemon juice
¹/2 teaspoon salt
¹/4 teaspoon freshly ground pepper
2 cups diced cooked turkey or chicken
2 red apples, cored and diced
²/3 cup sliced celery
¹/2 cup chopped walnuts

In large bowl combine mayonnaise, lemon juice, salt
and pepper. Add turkey, apples and celery; toss to
coat well. Cover; chill. Just before serving, sprinkle
with walnuts.

Hot & Spicy Glazed Carrots

Hot & Spicy Glazed Carrots

Makes 4 servings

- 2 tablespoons vegetable oil
- 2 dried red chili peppers
- 1 pound carrots, peeled and cut diagonally into
  1/8-inch slices
- 1/4 cup KIKKOMAN® Teriyaki Baste & Glaze

Heat oil in hot wok or large skillet over high heat. Add peppers and stir-fry until darkened; remove and discard. Add carrots; reduce heat to medium. Stir-fry 4 minutes, or until tender-crisp. Stir in teriyaki baste & glaze and cook until carrots are glazed. Serve immediately.

Scalloped Potatoes Nokkelost®

Makes 8 servings

- 1 cup chopped leeks
- 1/4 cup (1/2 stick) butter or margarine
- 1/4 cup all-purpose flour
- 1 1/2 teaspoons salt
- 1/8 teaspoon pepper
- 2 cups milk
- 8 cups sliced red-skinned potatoes, unpeeled
- 2 cups shredded NOKKELOST® cheese
- 3/4 cup bread crumbs
- 1/4 melted butter or margarine

In saucepan, cook leeks in 1/4 cup butter until tender. Stir in flour, salt and pepper. Gradually stir in milk. Cook, stirring until thickened. In 2-quart buttered baking dish, layer half of the potatoes, half of the leek sauce and half of the cheese. Repeat layering. Bake, covered, at 375°F for 45 minutes. Uncover. Blend bread crumbs and melted butter. Sprinkle around edge of casserole. Bake 15 minutes longer.

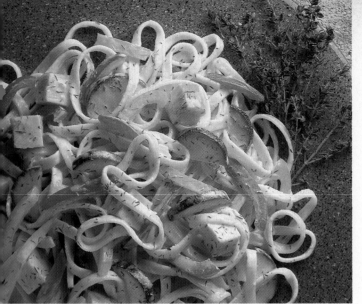

Smoked Turkey & Pepper Pasta Salad

Smoked Turkey & Pepper Pasta Salad

Makes about 6 servings

¾ cup MIRACLE WHIP® Salad Dressing
1 tablespoon dijon mustard
½ teaspoon dried thyme leaves
8 ozs. fettucini, cooked, drained
1 cup (8 ozs.) diced LOUIS RICH® Smoked
    Boneless Turkey Breast
¾ cup zucchini slices, cut into halves
½ cup red bell pepper strips
½ cup yellow bell pepper strips
    Salt and black pepper

Mix salad dressing, mustard and thyme until well blended. Add pasta, turkey and vegetables; mix lightly. Season with salt and pepper to taste. Chill. Add additional dressing before serving, if desired.

Preparation time: 15 minutes plus chilling

Pineapple Lime Mold

Makes 8 servings

1 can (20 oz.) DOLE® Pineapple Chunks
2 pkgs. (3 oz. each) lime gelatin
2 cups boiling water
1 cup dairy sour cream
½ cup chopped walnuts
½ cup chopped celery

Drain pineapple, reserve syrup. Dissolve gelatin in boiling water. Add sour cream and reserved syrup. Chill until slightly thickened. Stir in pineapple, walnuts and celery. Pour into 7-cup mold. Chill until set.

Sweet Potato Salad

Makes 6 servings

2 pounds sweet potatoes, peeled and cubed
2 tablespoons lemon juice
1 cup HELLMANN'S® or BEST FOODS® Real,
    Light or Cholesterol Free Reduced Calorie
    Mayonnaise
1 teaspoon grated orange peel
2 tablespoons orange juice
1 tablespoon honey
1 teaspoon chopped fresh ginger
¼ teaspoon salt
⅛ teaspoon nutmeg
1 cup coarsely chopped pecans
1 cup sliced celery
⅓ cup chopped pitted dates
    Lettuce leaves
1 can (11 ounces) mandarin orange sections,
    drained

In medium saucepan cook potatoes 8 to 10 minutes in boiling, salted water just until tender. (Do not overcook.) Drain. Toss with lemon juice. In large bowl combine mayonnaise, orange peel, orange juice, honey, ginger, salt and nutmeg. Stir in warm potatoes, pecans, celery and dates. Cover; chill. To serve, spoon salad onto lettuce-lined platter. Arrange orange sections around salad. Garnish as desired.

Homestead Succotash

Makes 6 to 8 servings

¼ lb. bacon, diced
1 cup chopped onion
½ teaspoon thyme
1 can (17 oz.) DEL MONTE® Whole Kernel
    Golden Sweet Corn, drained
1 can (17 oz.) DEL MONTE® Green Lima
    Beans, drained

In skillet, cook bacon until crisp; drain. Add onion and thyme; cook until tender. Stir in vegetables and heat through.

Microwave: In shallow 1-quart microwavable dish, cook bacon on high 6 minutes or until crisp; drain. Add onion and thyme; cover and cook on high 2 to 3 minutes or until tender. Add vegetables. Cover and cook on high 3 to 4 minutes or until heated through.

Total time for conventional method: 13 minutes

Sweet Potato Salad

Harvest Sausage Stuffing

Makes about 3 quarts

1 pound bulk sausage
2 cups chopped celery
8 ounces fresh mushrooms, sliced (about 2 cups)
1½ cups chopped onion
4 teaspoons WYLER'S® or STEERO® Chicken-Flavor Instant Bouillon *or* 4 Chicken-Flavor Bouillon Cubes
1 to 1½ cups boiling water
2 (7-ounce) packages herb-seasoned stuffing mix
1⅓ cups (one-half jar) NONE SUCH® Ready-to-Use Mincemeat
1 (8-ounce) can sliced water chestnuts, coarsely chopped
2 teaspoons poultry seasoning

In large skillet, brown sausage; pour off fat. Add celery, mushrooms and onion; cook until onion is tender. Add bouillon and water to sausage mixture; bring to a boil. In large bowl, combine remaining ingredients with sausage mixture; mix well. Use to loosely stuff turkey just before roasting. Place remaining stuffing in 2-quart greased baking dish; cover. Bake at 350°F for 45 minutes or until hot. Refrigerate leftovers.

Harvest Sausage Stuffing

Gorgonzola Green Bean Salad

Makes 4 servings

⅓ cup Gorgonzola or blue cheese
3 tablespoons olive oil
2 tablespoons red wine vinegar
1 can (16 oz.) DEL MONTE® Blue Lake Cut Green Beans, drained
1 cup cherry tomatoes, halved
½ cup chopped walnuts
¼ cup sliced green onions
  Romaine lettuce, optional
  Salt and pepper

In bowl, mash cheese with oil and vinegar. Toss with beans, tomatoes, nuts and onions. Serve on a bed of romaine lettuce, if desired. Add salt and pepper to taste.

Total time: 10 minutes

Sea Breeze Fish Salad

Makes 4 servings

1 pound firm white fish fillets (red snapper, sea bass or orange roughy), about 1 inch thick
1³/₄ cups water
1 tablespoon grated lemon peel
6 tablespoons lemon juice, divided
3 tablespoons **KIKKOMAN®** Lite Soy Sauce, divided
6 ounces fresh snow peas, trimmed and cut diagonally into 1-inch pieces
2 tablespoons vegetable oil
1 tablespoon minced onion
¹/₂ teaspoon thyme, crumbled
¹/₄ teaspoon sugar
¹/₂ medium cantaloupe, chunked
1 tablespoon minced fresh cilantro or parsley

Cut fish into 1-inch cubes. Combine water, lemon peel, 4 tablespoons lemon juice and 1 tablespoon lite soy sauce in large skillet. Heat only until mixture starts to simmer. Add fish; simmer, uncovered, 3 minutes, or until fish flakes easily when tested with fork. Remove fish with slotted spoon to plate. Cool slightly; cover and refrigerate 1 hour, or until thoroughly chilled. Meanwhile, cook snow peas in boiling water 2 minutes, or until tender-crisp; cool under cold water and drain thoroughly. Chill. Measure remaining 2 tablespoons lemon juice and 2 tablespoons lite soy sauce, oil, onion, thyme and sugar into jar with screw-top lid; cover and shake well. Combine peas, cantaloupe and cilantro in large bowl; add dressing and toss to coat all ingredients. Add fish and gently stir to combine. Serve immediately.

Christmas Ribbon

Christmas Ribbon

Makes 12 servings

2 packages (4-serving size each) *or* 1 package (8-serving size) **JELL-O®** Brand Gelatin, Strawberry Flavor
5 cups boiling water
²/₃ cup sour cream *or* plain or vanilla yogurt
2 packages (4-serving size each) *or* 1 package (8-serving size) **JELL-O®** Brand Gelatin, Lime Flavor

Dissolve strawberry flavor gelatin in 2¹/₂ cups of the boiling water. Pour 1¹/₂ cups gelatin into 6-cup ring mold. Chill until set but not firm, about 30 minutes. Chill remaining gelatin in bowl until slightly thickened; gradually blend in ¹/₃ cup of the sour cream. Spoon over gelatin in mold. Chill until set but not firm, about 15 minutes.

Repeat with lime flavor gelatin, remaining 2¹/₂ cups boiling water and ¹/₃ cup sour cream, chilling dissolved gelatin before measuring and pouring into mold. Chill at least 2 hours. Unmold.

Preparation time: 30 minutes
Chill time: 3 hours

Apple Praline Squash

Apple Praline Squash

Makes 4 servings

2 medium acorn squash, halved lengthwise,
    seeds removed
$1/2$ cup water
$1/4$ cup **LAND O LAKES®** Unsalted Butter
1 large cooking apple, cored, cut into $3/4$-inch
    pieces
$1/3$ cup firmly packed brown sugar
$1/4$ teaspoon cinnamon
2 teaspoons vanilla
2 tablespoons chopped pecans

Heat oven to 400°F. In 13×9-inch baking pan place
squash cut side up; pour water into pan. Cover with
aluminum foil. Bake for 40 to 50 minutes or until
tender. In 8-inch skillet melt butter. Stir in apple,
brown sugar, cinnamon and vanilla. Cook over
medium heat, stirring constantly, until apples are
crisp-tender (3 to 4 minutes). Spoon an equal
amount into each baked squash half; sprinkle with
pecans.

Candied Sweet Potatoes

Makes 6 servings

1 cup **DOMINO® BROWNULATED®** Light
    Brown Sugar
    Grated rind and juice of 1 navel orange
2 tablespoons butter or margarine
6 medium sweet potatoes, parboiled, peeled and
    halved lengthwise

In large skillet, combine sugar, grated rind, orange
juice and butter. Heat, stirring occasionally, over
medium heat until blended and smooth. Add
potatoes and simmer, uncovered, for 20 minutes.
Baste and turn potatoes occasionally to glaze evenly.

Mandarin Orange and Red Onion Salad

Makes 4 to 6 servings

1 cup **BLUE DIAMOND®** Sliced Natural
    Almonds
1 tablespoon butter
2 tablespoons lemon juice
1 teaspoon Dijon mustard
$1/2$ teaspoon sugar
$1/2$ teaspoon salt
$1/4$ teaspoon white pepper
$1/2$ cup vegetable oil
1 head romaine lettuce, torn into pieces
1 can (11 ounces) mandarin orange segments,
    drained
1 small red onion, thinly sliced

Sauté almonds in butter until golden; reserve.
Combine next 5 ingredients. Whisk in oil. Combine
lettuce, oranges, onion, and almonds. Toss with
dressing.

Spinach Squares

Makes 8 to 10 servings

1 10-oz. pkg. frozen chopped spinach, cooked,
    well drained
$1/3$ cup chopped onion
$1/3$ cup chopped red pepper
$1/2$ lb. **VELVEETA®** Pasteurized Process Cheese
    Spread, cubed
2 cups cooked rice
3 eggs, beaten
$1/8$ teaspoon pepper

In large bowl, combine ingredients; spoon into
greased 10×6-inch baking dish. Bake at 350°F, 25
minutes. Let stand 5 minutes before serving. Cut
into squares.

Preparation time: 10 minutes
Baking time: 25 minutes plus standing

Mandarin Orange and Red Onion Salad

Mandarin Orange and Red Onion Salad

1 cup Blue Diamond
Almonds
1 tablespoon butter
2 tablespoons lemon
1 teaspoon

Fruited Rice Pilaf

Fruited Rice Pilaf

Makes 4 servings

2½ cups water
  1 cup uncooked rice
  2 tablespoons butter or margarine
  1 medium tomato, chopped
  ⅓ cup minced dried apples
  ¼ cup minced dried apricots
  ¼ cup sliced green onions
  ¾ teaspoon LAWRY'S® Seasoned Salt
  ¼ teaspoon LAWRY'S® Garlic Powder with
      Parsley
  3 tablespoons sliced almonds

In 2-quart saucepan, bring water to a boil; add rice and butter. Return to a boil. Reduce heat; cover and simmer 15 minutes. Add remaining ingredients except almonds; cook 5 to 10 minutes longer or until rice is tender. Stir in almonds.

Presentation: Garnish with apple slices and celery leaves. Serve with baked pork chops, roasted meats or poultry.
Hint: For variety and added flavor, try adding ¼ teaspoon curry powder to cooked rice.

Honey Mustard Peas

Makes 4 servings

½ cup coarsely chopped onion
¼ cup julienne carrots
  1 tablespoon butter or margarine
  1 tablespoon honey
  1 tablespoon Dijon mustard
  1 can (17 oz.) DEL MONTE® Sweet Peas,
    drained

In saucepan, cook onion and carrots in butter until tender. Blend in honey and mustard. Stir in peas; heat through.

Microwave Directions: In 1-quart microwavable dish, combine onion, carrots and butter. Cover and cook on high 4 minutes or until tender. Stir in honey and mustard. Stir in peas. Cook on high 1 minute.

Total time for conventional method: 10 minutes

Old-Fashioned Bread Stuffing

Makes 8 cups (enough for 12- to 14-pound turkey)

1 1/2 cups chopped onion
1 1/2 cups diced celery
  1 stick (1/2 cup) butter or margarine
  1 teaspoon poultry seasoning
  1 teaspoon rubbed sage
  1 teaspoon salt
    Dash ground black pepper
 1/2 cup water or chicken broth
  8 cups dried bread cubes (10 to 12 bread slices,
    cubed and dried overnight)

Cook and stir onion and celery in butter in medium skillet over medium heat until tender. Stir in seasonings. Add onion mixture and water to bread cubes in large bowl. Toss to mix. Stuff neck and body cavities of BUTTERBALL® turkey. Roast immediately.

Cranberry-Sausage: Cut 1 cup fresh cranberries into halves. Cut 1 package (8 ounces) fully cooked sausage links into pieces. Add to bread cubes.

Bacon and Green Pepper: Substitute 1 1/2 cups chopped green bell pepper for celery. Substitute 1 teaspoon dried thyme leaves, crushed, for poultry seasoning and sage. Reduce salt to 1/2 teaspoon. Add 12 slices cooked diced bacon to bread cubes.

Classic Waldorf Salad

Makes about 8 servings

 1/2 cup HELLMANN'S® or BEST FOODS® Real,
    Light or Cholesterol Free Reduced Calorie
    Mayonnaise
  1 tablespoon sugar
  1 tablespoon lemon juice
 1/8 teaspoon salt
  3 medium-size red apples, cored and diced
  1 cup sliced celery
 1/2 cup chopped walnuts

In medium bowl combine mayonnaise, sugar, lemon juice and salt. Add apples and celery; toss to coat well. Cover; chill. Just before serving, sprinkle with walnuts.

Turkey Salad with Pita Bread

Makes 6 servings

  3 cups cubed cooked BUTTERBALL® turkey
    (1 pound)
  1 cup sour cream
  3 green onions, sliced
  1 tablespoon dried dill weed
  1 teaspoon seasoned salt
  1 medium cucumber, sliced thin
  1 small red onion, sliced thin
 12 small cherry tomatoes, cut into halves
 12 small fresh mushrooms, sliced thin
    Lettuce leaves
  6 pita breads, 6 1/2-inch diameter, cut into halves

Blend sour cream, green onions, dill weed and salt in medium bowl. Add turkey and vegetables except lettuce; toss to combine. Serve on lettuce with pita bread. Or fill pita bread halves with turkey mixture and serve as sandwiches.

Turkey Salad with Pita Bread

Savory Lemon Vegetables

"Lite" Apricot Stuffing

Makes 8 servings

1 cup sliced celery
¾ cup chopped onion
1½ cups turkey broth or reduced-sodium chicken bouillon
16 slices reduced-calorie bread, cubed and dried
2 tablespoons parsley flakes
1½ teaspoons poultry seasoning
½ teaspoon salt
2 egg whites
¼ cup dried apricots, chopped

In small saucepan, over medium-high heat, combine celery, onion and turkey broth; bring to a boil. Reduce heat to low; cover and simmer 5 minutes or until vegetables are tender. In large bowl, combine celery mixture, bread cubes, parsley, poultry seasoning, salt, egg whites and apricots. Spoon into lightly greased 2-quart casserole; cover. Bake at 350°F 30 minutes or until heated through.

Favorite Recipe from **National Turkey Federation**

Savory Lemon Vegetables

Makes 8 servings

6 slices bacon, cooked and crumbled, reserving ¼ cup drippings
1 pound carrots, pared and sliced
1 medium head cauliflower, core removed
1 cup finely chopped onion
½ cup REALEMON® Lemon Juice from Concentrate
½ cup water
4 teaspoons sugar
1 teaspoon salt
1 teaspoon thyme leaves
Chopped parsley

In large saucepan, cook carrots and cauliflower in small amount of water until tender. Meanwhile, in medium skillet, cook onion in reserved drippings. Add ReaLemon® brand, *½ cup* water, sugar, salt and thyme; bring to a boil. Drain vegetables; arrange on serving dish. Pour warm sauce over vegetables. Garnish with bacon and parsley.

Microwave: Cook bacon, reserving *¼ cup* drippings. On large microwavable platter with rim, arrange carrots and cauliflower. Cover with plastic wrap; cook on 100% power (high) 14 to 16 minutes. In 1-quart glass measure, cook reserved bacon drippings and onion on 100% power (high) 1 minute. Add ReaLemon® brand, water, sugar, salt and thyme. Cook on 100% power (high) 5½ to 6 minutes or until sauce boils. Proceed as above.

Creamy Italian Pasta Salad

Makes about 6 servings

1 cup HELLMANN'S® or BEST FOODS® Real, Light or Cholesterol Free Reduced Calorie Mayonnaise
2 tablespoons red wine vinegar
1 clove garlic, minced
1 tablespoon chopped fresh basil *or* 1 teaspoon dried basil
1 teaspoon salt
¼ teaspoon freshly ground black pepper
1½ cups twist or spiral pasta, cooked, rinsed with cold water and drained
1 cup quartered cherry tomatoes
½ cup coarsely chopped green pepper
½ cup slivered pitted ripe olives

In large bowl combine mayonnaise, vinegar, garlic, basil, salt and pepper. Stir in pasta, cherry tomatoes, green pepper and olives. Cover; chill.

Beet and Pear Salad

Makes 4 to 6 servings

1 can (16 oz.) **DEL MONTE®** Bartlett Pear
    Halves
1 can (16 oz.) **DEL MONTE®** Sliced Beets,
    drained
½ cup thinly sliced red onion
2 tablespoons vegetable oil
1 tablespoon white wine vinegar
⅓ cup crumbled blue cheese
    Lettuce leaves, optional

Drain pears reserving 1 tablespoon syrup. Cut pears
in half lengthwise. Place pears, beets and onion in
medium bowl. Whisk together oil, vinegar and
reserved syrup. Pour over salad; toss gently. Just
before serving, add cheese and toss. Serve on bed of
lettuce leaves, if desired.

Total time: 10 minutes

Sweet Potato-Cranberry Bake

Makes 4 to 6 servings

1 can (40 ounces) whole sweet potatoes, drained
1 can (2.8 ounces) **DURKEE®** French Fried
    Onions
2 cups fresh cranberries
2 tablespoons packed brown sugar
⅓ cup honey

Preheat oven to 400°F. In 1½-quart casserole, layer
sweet potatoes, *½ can* French Fried Onions and *1 cup*
cranberries. Sprinkle with brown sugar; drizzle with
half the honey. Top with remaining cranberries and
honey. Bake, covered, for 35 minutes or until heated
through. Gently stir casserole. Top with remaining
onions; bake, uncovered, 1 to 3 minutes or until
onions are golden brown.

Beet and Pear Salad

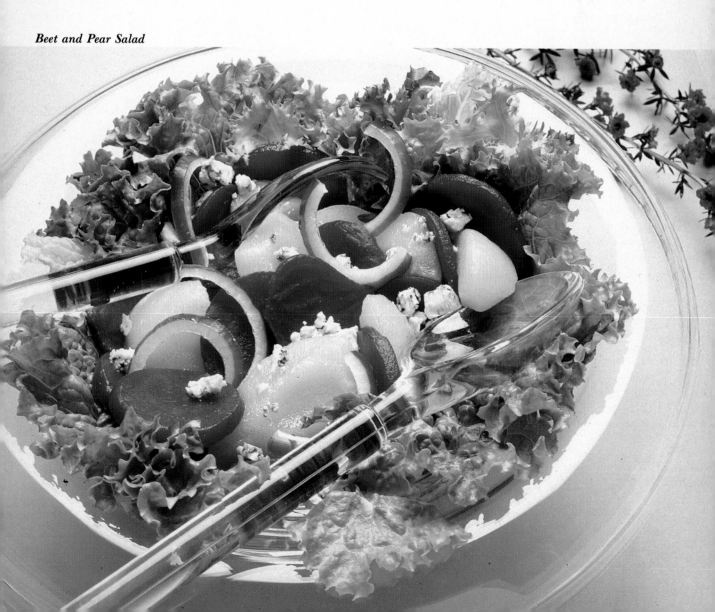

Main Dishes

Roasted Turkey with Savory Cranberry Stuffing

Makes 10 to 12 servings

1 cup chopped celery
1 cup chopped onion
1/2 cup margarine or butter
1 (16-ounce) can whole berry cranberry sauce
2 tablespoons WYLER'S® or STEERO®
    Chicken-Flavor Instant Bouillon *or*
    6 Chicken-Flavor Bouillon Cubes
12 cups dry bread cubes (about 16 slices)
1 cup chopped pecans
2 teaspoons poultry seasoning
1 teaspoon rubbed sage
3 cups hot water
1 (12- to 14-pound) turkey, thawed if frozen
    Vegetable oil

In large skillet, cook celery and onion in margarine until tender; add cranberry sauce and bouillon. Cook and stir until bouillon dissolves. In large bowl, combine bread cubes, pecans, seasonings and water; add cranberry mixture. Mix well.

Preheat oven to 325°F. Remove neck and giblets from turkey cavities. Rinse turkey; drain well. Stuff neck and body cavities lightly with stuffing. Place extra stuffing in greased baking dish. Cover; refrigerate. Turn wings back to hold neck skin in place. Place turkey, breast side up, on flat rack in open pan. Insert meat thermometer into thickest part of thigh next to body, not touching bone. Brush skin with oil. Place turkey in oven and roast about 4 hours. (Bake extra stuffing with turkey during last 40 minutes or until hot.) When skin is golden brown, shield breast loosely with foil to prevent overbrowning. Check for doneness; thigh temperature should be 180° to 185°F. Let turkey stand 15 to 20 minutes before carving. Refrigerate leftovers.

Rich Turkey Gravy: In medium skillet, stir 1/4 to 1/3 cup flour into 1/4 cup pan drippings; cook and stir until dark brown. Stir in 2 cups hot water and 2 teaspoons WYLER'S® or STEERO® Chicken-Flavor Instant Bouillon *or* 2 Chicken-Flavor Bouillon Cubes; cook and stir until thickened and bouillon is dissolved. Refrigerate leftovers. Makes about 1 1/2 cups.

Ham in Peach Sauce

Makes 10 servings

1 can (5 lbs.) fully-cooked ham
    Whole cloves
2 cans (16 oz. each) DEL MONTE® Yellow
    Cling Sliced Peaches, drained
1 jar (10 oz.) apricot preserves
1 cup dry sherry
1 teaspoon grated orange peel
1/4 teaspoon allspice

Place ham in 13×9×2-inch baking dish. Score ham and insert cloves. In food processor or blender container, process remaining ingredients until smooth. Pour over ham. Bake at 325°F, 1 hour, basting occasionally. Remove ham to serving platter; serve with sauce. Garnish with lemon slices and parsley, if desired. Can be served hot or cold.

Roasted Turkey with Savory Cranberry Stuffing

Baked Salmon with Almonds and Lime-Parsley Sauce

Baked Salmon with Almonds and Lime-Parsley Sauce

Makes 4 to 6 servings

1 large clove garlic, chopped finely
1 egg yolk
1 teaspoon lime juice
1/2 teaspoon cumin
  Salt
  White pepper
1/2 cup vegetable oil
4 1/2 teaspoons olive oil, divided
6 tablespoons chopped parsley
4 salmon fillets, about 6 ounces each
3/4 cup **BLUE DIAMOND®** Sliced Natural
  Almonds, lightly toasted

In food processor or blender, combine garlic, egg yolk, lime juice, cumin, 1/4 teaspoon salt, and a pinch pepper. With machine running, *slowly* pour in vegetable oil and 1 1/2 teaspoons olive oil. (To prepare by hand, beat egg yolk until thick and lemon colored. Beat in garlic, lime juice, cumin, 1/4 teaspoon salt, and a pinch pepper. Combine vegetable oil and 1 1/2 teaspoons olive oil. Whisking constantly, add oils *one drop at a time* until mixture begins to thicken. Pour remaining oil in a thin, steady stream, whisking constantly.) Mixture will resemble mayonnaise. Fold in chopped parsley. Brush salmon with remaining 3 teaspoons olive oil; season with salt and pepper. Spread parsley sauce down center of each fillet. Top with almonds. Bake at 400°F for 8 to 12 minutes or until fish is just firm.

Beef Burgundy

Makes 6³/4 cups or 6 servings

2 pounds beef for stew, cut into 1 1/2-inch pieces
1/4 cup all-purpose flour
4 slices bacon, diced
  Vegetable oil
2 medium cloves garlic, minced
12 ounces small whole white onions
1 package (8 ounces) **CAMPBELL'S FRESH®**
  mushrooms
1 tablespoon chopped fresh thyme leaves *or*
  1 teaspoon dried thyme leaves, crushed
1 tablespoon tomato paste
2 cups Burgundy or other dry red wine
1 can (14 1/2 ounces) **SWANSON®** clear ready to
  serve beef broth
1 medium bay leaf
  Coarsely ground pepper
  Hot cooked noodles
  Chopped fresh parsley for garnish

On waxed paper, coat beef with flour; set aside. In 4-quart Dutch oven over medium heat, cook bacon until browned. With slotted spoon, remove bacon; set aside.

In drippings over medium-high heat, cook beef a few pieces at a time, until browned on all sides. Remove beef as it browns. Add vegetable oil if necessary. Add garlic, onions, mushrooms and thyme to hot drippings; cook until mushrooms and onions are lightly browned, stirring occasionally. Remove from Dutch oven; set aside.

Return beef and bacon to Dutch oven. Add tomato paste, wine, broth and bay leaf; heat to boiling. Reduce heat to low. Cover; simmer 1 hour. Add mushroom mixture; cover and cook 30 minutes more or until beef and onions are fork-tender. Simmer, uncovered, until slightly thickened, about 10 minutes. Remove bay leaf. Season with pepper. Serve over noodles; garnish with parsley.

Pinwheel Meat Loaf

Makes about 8 servings

- ½ cup milk
- 1½ cups crustless Italian or French bread cubes
- 1½ pounds ground beef
- ½ pound sweet Italian sausage, removed from casings and crumbled
- 2 eggs, slightly beaten
- 2 tablespoons finely chopped parsley
- 1 tablespoon finely chopped garlic
- 1 teaspoon salt
- ½ teaspoon pepper
- 2 cups water
- 1 tablespoon butter or margarine
- 1 package LIPTON® Rice & Sauce–Cajun-Style
- 2 packages (10 ounces each) frozen chopped spinach, thawed and squeezed dry

In large bowl, pour milk over bread cubes, then mash with fork until bread is soaked. Thoroughly combine bread mixture with ground beef, sausage, eggs, parsley, garlic, salt and pepper. Place on 12×12-inch sheet of aluminum foil moistened with water.

Cover with 12×14-inch sheet of waxed paper moistened with water. Using hands or rolling pin, press into 12×12-inch square. Refrigerate 2 hours or until well chilled.

In medium saucepan, bring water, butter and rice & Cajun-style sauce to a boil. Continue boiling over medium heat, stirring occasionally, 10 minutes or until rice is tender. Refrigerate 2 hours or until well chilled.

Preheat oven to 350°F. Remove waxed paper from ground beef mixture. If desired, season spinach with additional salt and pepper. Spread spinach over ground beef mixture leaving 1-inch border. Spread rice evenly over spinach. Roll, starting at long end and using foil as a guide, jelly-roll style, removing foil while rolling; seal edges tightly. In 13×9-inch baking pan, place meat loaf seam-side down. Bake 1 hour or until done. Let stand 15 minutes before serving. Cut into 1-inch slices.

Pinwheel Meat Loaf

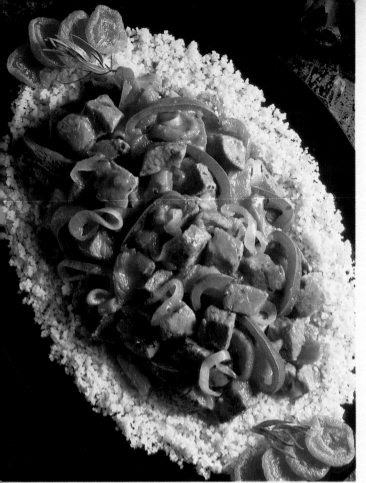
Savory Lamb with Couscous

Savory Lamb with Couscous

Makes 6 servings

1½ pounds lean boneless lamb shoulder, cut into
    1-inch cubes
1 tablespoon vegetable oil
¾ cup chopped onions
2 cloves garlic, minced
1 tablespoon dried tarragon leaves, crushed
1½ cups tomato juice
1 medium green pepper, cut into strips
¾ cup dried apricots, halved
1 cup **NEAR EAST®** Couscous
1 tablespoon butter
    Dried apricots (optional)
    Fresh tarragon (optional)

In large skillet, brown lamb in oil. Add onions, garlic and dried tarragon; cook until onions are tender-crisp. Drain fat. Stir in tomato juice, green pepper and the ¾ cup apricots. Cover; simmer 15 to 20 minutes or until lamb is cooked. Prepare couscous according to package directions using only 1 tablespoon butter. Fluff couscous lightly with fork; spoon onto platter. Top with lamb mixture. Garnish with dried apricots and fresh tarragon.

Easy Paella

Makes 4 servings

1 medium onion, cut into halves and chopped
1 large red or green bell pepper, sliced
1 clove garlic, minced
2 tablespoons vegetable oil
1 can (16 ounces) tomatoes with juice, cut up
1 package (10 ounces) frozen artichoke hearts,
    cut into quarters
½ cup dry white wine
½ teaspoon dried thyme, crushed
¼ teaspoon salt
⅛ teaspoon saffron or turmeric
2 cups cooked rice
1 cup frozen peas
1 can (6½ ounces) **STARKIST®** Tuna, drained
    and broken into chunks
½ pound large shrimp, peeled and deveined

In a large skillet sauté onion, bell pepper and garlic in oil for 3 minutes. Stir in tomatoes with juice, artichoke hearts, wine and seasonings. Bring to a boil; reduce heat. Simmer for 10 minutes. Stir in rice, peas, tuna and shrimp. Cook for 3 to 5 minutes more, or until shrimp turn pink and mixture is heated.

Preparation time: 30 minutes

Calorie count: 382 calories per serving.

Strawberry Glazed Ham

Makes 8 to 10 servings

1 (5- to 7-pound) fully-cooked smoked butt or
    shank-half ham
1½ cups **SMUCKER'S®** Simply Fruit Strawberry
⅓ cup prepared mustard
¼ cup lemon juice

Trim skin from ham. With sharp knife, score fat surface, making uniform diagonal cuts about ⅛-inch deep and ¾-inch apart. Place ham fat side up on a rack in a shallow roasting pan; bake in 325°F oven 1¾ to 2½ hours. Meanwhile, in a small saucepan, combine fruit spread, mustard and lemon juice; cook over low heat, stirring, until blended. During last 20 minutes of baking time, brush ham with about ½ cup strawberry glaze. Let ham stand 10 minutes for easier slicing. Heat remaining glaze and serve as a sauce for the ham.

Easy Paella

Turkey with Mushroom Stuffing and Mushroom Gravy

Turkey with Mushroom Stuffing

Makes 10 to 12 servings

¼ cup butter or margarine
1 package (8 ounces) **CAMPBELL'S FRESH®** mushrooms, coarsely chopped
1 package (8 ounces) **PEPPERIDGE FARM®** herb seasoned stuffing
1 cup **SWANSON®** clear ready to serve chicken broth
½ cup chopped fresh parsley
1 teaspoon grated lemon peel
⅛ teaspoon pepper
1 (10- to 12-pound) ready-to-stuff turkey
Mushroom Gravy (recipe follows)

To prepare stuffing: In 10-inch skillet over medium heat, in hot butter, cook mushrooms until tender, stirring occasionally. In large bowl, toss together stuffing, mushrooms, broth, parsley, lemon peel and pepper. Remove giblets and neck from inside turkey. Rinse turkey with cold running water; drain well. Spoon stuffing mixture lightly into neck and body cavities. Fold skin over stuffing; skewer closed. Tie legs. On rack in roasting pan, place turkey breast-side up. Insert meat thermometer into thickest part

of meat between breast and thigh, not touching bone. Roast, uncovered, at 325°F for 3½ hours or until internal temperature reaches 180°F and drumstick moves easily. Baste occasionally with pan drippings. When skin turns golden, cover loosely with tent of foil. Serve with Mushroom Gravy.

Mushroom Gravy

3 to 4 tablespoons poultry drippings
1 package (8 ounces) **CAMPBELL'S FRESH®** mushrooms, sliced (about 3 cups)
¼ cup all-purpose flour
2 cups **SWANSON®** clear ready to serve chicken broth
1 cup milk
  Salt
  Pepper

In 10-inch skillet or roasting pan over medium heat, in hot drippings, cook mushrooms until tender and liquid is evaporated. Stir in flour until blended. Gradually stir in broth and milk. Cook until mixture boils and thickens, stirring often. Season with salt and pepper. Makes about 3 cups.

Sausage-Stuffed Cornish Hens

Makes 2 servings

½ pound bulk pork sausage
¼ pound mushrooms, sliced
2 cups STOVE TOP® Chicken Flavor Flexible
    Serving Stuffing Mix
¼ cup grated carrot
1 cup hot water
2 Cornish game hens (1 to 1½ pounds each)
    Vegetable oil
2 tablespoons apple jelly

Brown sausage and mushrooms in skillet; drain fat.
Mix in stuffing mix, carrot and water. Rinse hens
with cold water; pat dry. Spoon stuffing into cavities.
Skewer neck skin to back. Tie legs to tail and twist
wing tips under. Place birds breast side up in shallow
roasting pan. Brush with oil. Roast at 350°F for 1
hour. Spoon apple jelly over hens. Bake 10 minutes
longer. Place any remaining stuffing in casserole
dish. Cover; bake with hens during last 20 minutes
of baking time.

Marvelous Marinated London Broil

Makes 6 to 8 servings

½ cup HELLMANN'S® or BEST FOODS® Real,
    Light or Cholesterol Free Reduced Calorie
    Mayonnaise
⅓ cup soy sauce
¼ cup lemon juice
2 tablespoons prepared mustard
1 clove garlic, minced or pressed
½ teaspoon ground ginger
¼ teaspoon freshly ground pepper
1 beef top round steak (3 pounds), 2 inches
    thick

In large shallow dish combine mayonnaise, soy sauce,
lemon juice, mustard, garlic, ginger and pepper. Add
steak, turning to coat. Cover; marinate in
refrigerator several hours or overnight. Grill or broil
about 6 inches from heat, turning once, 25 to 30
minutes or until desired doneness. To serve, slice
diagonally across grain.

Pasta Roll-Ups

Makes 6 servings

1 package (1.5 ounces) LAWRY'S® Original-
    Style Spaghetti Sauce Spices & Seasonings
1 can (6 ounces) tomato paste
2¼ cups water
2 tablespoons butter or vegetable oil
2 cups cottage cheese or ricotta cheese
1 cup (4 ounces) grated mozzarella cheese
¼ cup grated Parmesan cheese
2 eggs, lightly beaten
½ to 1 teaspoon LAWRY'S® Garlic Salt
½ teaspoon dried basil, crushed (optional)
8 ounces lasagna noodles, cooked and drained

In medium saucepan, prepare Spaghetti Sauce Spices
& Seasonings according to package directions using
tomato paste, water and butter. In large bowl,
combine remaining ingredients except noodles; blend
well. Spread ¼ cup cheese mixture on entire length
of each lasagna noodle; roll up. Place noodles, seam-
side down, in microwave-safe baking dish. Cover
with vented plastic wrap and microwave on HIGH 6
to 7 minutes or until cheese begins to melt. Pour
sauce over rolls and microwave on HIGH 1 minute
longer, if necessary, to heat sauce.

Presentation: *Sprinkle with additional grated Parmesan
cheese. Garnish with fresh basil leaves.*

Hint: *For quick microwavable meals, wrap prepared rolls
individually and freeze. Sauce may be frozen in ¼ cup
servings.*

Pasta Roll-Ups

Fiesta Potato Bake

Fiesta Potato Bake

Makes 4 servings

2 cups cubed cooked BUTTERBALL® turkey
  (³/₄ pound)
6 medium (1¹/₂ pounds) potatoes, pared, sliced
  thin
3 tablespoons all-purpose flour
2 teaspoons seasoned salt
¹/₄ teaspoon ground black pepper
1 medium onion, sliced thin (about 1 cup)
1 cup diced green bell pepper
¹/₂ cup diced red bell pepper
¹/₂ cup milk
2 tablespoons butter or margarine

Preheat oven to 350°F. Place half of the turkey in buttered, deep 2-quart casserole. Cover with half of the potatoes. Sprinkle with 1 tablespoon flour and half of the salt and pepper. Top with half of the onion slices and half of the green and red peppers. Combine remaining 2 tablespoons flour with milk; pour half over layered ingredients. Repeat layers with potatoes, onions, remaining turkey, green and red peppers, salt and pepper. Pour remaining milk over top; dot with butter. Cover and bake in oven 45 minutes. Remove cover; bake an additional 30 minutes or until potatoes are done.

Shrimp Milano

Makes 4 to 6 servings

1 lb. frozen cleaned shrimp, cooked, drained
2 cups mushroom slices
1 cup green or red pepper strips
1 garlic clove, minced
¹/₄ cup PARKAY® Margarine
³/₄ lb. VELVEETA® Pasteurized Process Cheese
  Spread, cubed
³/₄ cup whipping cream
¹/₂ teaspoon dill weed
¹/₃ cup (1¹/₂ ozs.) KRAFT® 100% Grated
  Parmesan Cheese
8 ozs. fettucini, cooked, drained

In large skillet, saute shrimp, vegetables and garlic in margarine. Reduce heat to low. Add process cheese spread, cream and dill. Stir until process cheese spread is melted. Stir in parmesan cheese. Add fettucini; toss lightly.

Preparation time: 20 minutes
Cooking time: 15 minutes

Braised Duckling and Pears

Makes 3 to 4 servings

1 (4- to 5-pound) frozen duckling, thawed and
  quartered
1 can (16 oz.) pear halves in heavy syrup
¹/₃ cup KIKKOMAN® Stir-Fry Sauce
1 cinnamon stick, about 3 inches long

Wash duckling quarters; dry thoroughly with paper towels. Heat large skillet or Dutch oven over medium heat. Add duckling; brown slowly on both sides about 15 minutes, or until golden. Meanwhile, drain pears; reserve all syrup. Remove ¹/₄ cup pear syrup and combine with stir-fry sauce; set aside. Drain off fat from pan. Pour syrup mixture over duckling; add cinnamon stick. Cover and simmer 40 minutes, or until tender, turning quarters over once. Remove duckling to serving platter; keep warm. Remove and discard cinnamon stick. Pour drippings into measuring cup; skim off fat. Combine ¹/₂ cup drippings with 2 tablespoons reserved pear syrup; return to pan with pears. Gently bring to boil and cook until pears are heated through, stirring occasionally. Serve duckling with pears and sauce.

Crown Roast of Pork

Makes 8 servings

1 (6-pound) pork crown roast (12 to 16 small ribs)
¼ cup butter or margarine
1 package (12 ounces) CAMPBELL'S FRESH® mushrooms, sliced
½ cup thinly sliced celery
½ cup water
1 package (8 ounces) PEPPERIDGE FARM® corn bread stuffing
1 cup coarsely chopped apple
⅛ teaspoon ground allspice
⅓ cup apricot preserves, melted

In roasting pan, place roast, bones pointing up. Cover bone tips with small pieces of foil. Insert meat thermometer into thickest part of meat, not touching bone. Roast at 325°F for 1½ hours.

Meanwhile, to prepare stuffing: In 10-inch skillet over medium heat, in hot butter, cook mushrooms and celery until tender, stirring occasionally. Stir in water; heat to boiling. In large bowl, combine stuffing, apple and allspice. Pour mushroom mixture over stuffing mixture; toss to mix well. Spoon stuffing mixture into center of roast, mounding high. Cover stuffing with foil. Roast 1 hour more. Remove foil from stuffing. Brush melted preserves over roast. Roast 30 minutes more or until internal temperature reaches 170°F, brushing often with preserves. Let roast stand 15 minutes for easier carving. Remove foil from bones before serving.

Pecan Turkey Sauté with Warm Cranberry Sauce

Makes 4 servings

½ cup unseasoned dry bread crumbs
¼ cup ground pecans
½ teaspoon LAWRY'S® Garlic Powder with Parsley
½ teaspoon LAWRY'S® Seasoned Salt
1 pound turkey cutlets
3 eggs, beaten
3 tablespoons butter or margarine
1 can (8 ounces) jellied cranberry sauce or whole berry cranberry sauce
⅓ cup French salad dressing
3 tablespoons water
2 tablespoons chopped green onion

In pie plate, combine bread crumbs, pecans and seasonings; blend well. Dip each turkey cutlet in eggs, then coat both sides with crumb mixture. In large skillet, melt butter and brown turkey cutlets 5 minutes on each side or until cooked through. In small saucepan, combine cranberry sauce, salad dressing, water and onion; blend well. Gently heat until warmed through, about 5 minutes. Spoon warm cranberry sauce over cutlets.

Presentation: *Serve with mashed potatoes or stuffing.*

Spicy Tomato Chicken

Makes 4 servings

½ cup QUAKER® Oat Bran hot cereal, uncooked
1½ teaspoons thyme leaves, crushed
1½ teaspoons garlic powder
⅛ to ¼ teaspoon ground red pepper
2 egg whites
2 chicken breasts, split, boned, skinned (about ¾ lb.)
2 tablespoons vegetable oil
¼ cup dry white wine
1 can (8 oz.) low sodium tomato sauce
½ cup sliced green onions

In shallow dish, combine oat bran, thyme, garlic powder and red pepper. In another shallow dish, lightly beat egg whites. Pound each chicken breast between sheets of waxed paper to even thickness. Coat with oat bran mixture; shake off excess. Dip into egg whites, then coat again with oat bran mixture. Saute chicken in oil over medium heat about 6 minutes; turn. Cook an additional 6 to 8 minutes or until juices run clear when pierced with fork. Remove to serving platter; keep warm.

Increase heat to high; add wine, mixing well with drippings. Add tomato sauce and green onions; heat through. Pour over chicken just before serving. Garnish with sliced green onions, if desired.

Spicy Tomato Chicken

Pork Chops with Almond Plum Sauce

Pork Chops with Almond Plum Sauce

Makes 4 servings

1 cup water
6 tablespoons lemon juice
6 tablespoons soy sauce
4 cloves garlic, chopped finely
1 1/2 teaspoons cornstarch
1/4 teaspoon salt
1/2 teaspoon white pepper
 Pinch cayenne
4 pork chops, about 1 inch thick
1 tablespoon vegetable oil
2/3 cup plum jam
1/4 cup BLUE DIAMOND® Sliced Natural
 Almonds, lightly toasted
1/4 cup sliced green onion tops, for garnish

Combine first 8 ingredients. Marinate pork chops in mixture in refrigerator 1 hour or overnight. Remove pork chops, reserving marinade. Sauté pork chops in oil over high heat 2 to 3 minutes on each side or until golden brown. Remove and reserve. Add marinade and plum jam to pan. Cook over medium heat until mixture thickens and coats the back of a spoon, about 5 minutes. Return pork chops to pan in single layer. Simmer, covered, 5 to 7 minutes. Remove cover and continue cooking 3 to 4 minutes or until pork chops are just cooked through and tender. To serve, remove chops to serving plate; sprinkle 1 tablespoon almonds over each chop. Pour sauce over and sprinkle each chop with 1 tablespoon sliced green onion tops.

Zesty Zucchini Lasagna

Makes about 6 servings

1 pound ground beef
1 package (1.5 ounces) LAWRY'S® Original-
 Style Spaghetti Sauce Spices & Seasonings
1 can (6 ounces) tomato paste
1 3/4 cups water
2 tablespoons IMPERIAL® Margarine
1/2 teaspoon basil leaves
1/8 teaspoon thyme leaves
2 cups ricotta cheese
1 egg, slightly beaten
4 medium zucchini, thinly sliced lengthwise
1 cup shredded mozzarella cheese (about
 4 ounces)

Preheat oven to 350°F. In medium saucepan, brown ground beef until no longer pink; drain. Into saucepan, stir in Spaghetti Sauce Spices & Seasonings, tomato paste, water, margarine, basil and thyme. Bring to a boil, then simmer uncovered 10 minutes. In small bowl, combine ricotta cheese with egg; set aside. In medium saucepan, bring 1 quart water to a boil. Add zucchini and cook 2 minutes; remove and rinse under cold running water. In 12×8-inch casserole, layer 1/2 of the zucchini, ricotta mixture and meat sauce. Repeat layers. Top with mozzarella cheese and bake uncovered 30 minutes or until cheese is melted.

Louisiana Chicken

Makes 4 servings

4 chicken breast halves, skinned and boned
2 cans (14 1/2 oz. each) DEL MONTE® Cajun
 Style Stewed Tomatoes
2 tablespoons cornstarch
4 slices Monterey Jack cheese
 Parsley

Place chicken in baking dish. Cover and bake at 375°F, 30 to 35 minutes; drain. Combine tomatoes and cornstarch in saucepan; stir to dissolve cornstarch. Cook, stirring constantly, until thickened. Remove chicken from baking dish. Pour all but 1 cup sauce into dish. Arrange chicken over sauce in dish; top with remaining sauce. Place 1 slice cheese on each piece of chicken. Bake until cheese melts. Garnish with parsley. Serve with hot cooked rice, if desired.

Spicy Sichuan Pork Stew

Makes 6 servings

2 pounds boneless pork shoulder (Boston butt)
1/4 cup all-purpose flour
2 tablespoons vegetable oil
1 3/4 cups water, divided
1/4 cup **KIKKOMAN®** Soy Sauce
3 tablespoons dry sherry
2 cloves garlic, pressed
1 teaspoon minced fresh ginger root
1/2 teaspoon crushed red pepper
1/4 teaspoon fennel seed, crushed
8 green onions and tops, cut into 1-inch lengths, separating whites from tops
2 large carrots, chunked
Hot cooked rice

Cut pork into 1-inch cubes. Coat in flour; reserve 2 tablespoons flour. Heat oil in Dutch oven or large pan over medium-high heat; brown pork on all sides in hot oil. Add 1 1/2 cups water, soy sauce, sherry, garlic, ginger, red pepper, fennel and white parts of green onions. Cover pan; bring to boil. Reduce heat and simmer 30 minutes. Add carrots; simmer, covered, 30 minutes longer, or until pork and carrots are tender. Meanwhile, combine reserved flour and remaining 1/4 cup water; set aside. Stir green onion tops into pork mixture; simmer 1 minute. Add flour mixture; bring to boil. Cook and stir until mixture is slightly thickened. Serve over rice.

Spicy Sichuan Pork Stew

Seafood over Angel Hair Pasta

Makes about 4 servings

1/4 cup **WISH-BONE®** Italian Dressing*
1/4 cup chopped shallots or onions
1 cup thinly sliced carrots
4 ounces snow peas, thinly sliced (about 1 cup)
1 cup chicken broth
1/4 cup sherry
1/2 pound uncooked medium shrimp, cleaned (keep tails on)
1/2 pound sea scallops
8 mussels, well scrubbed
1/4 cup whipping or heavy cream
2 tablespoons all-purpose flour
Salt and pepper to taste
8 ounces angel hair pasta or capellini, cooked and drained

In 12-inch skillet, heat Italian dressing and cook shallots over medium-high heat 2 minutes. Add carrots and snow peas and cook 2 minutes. Add broth, then sherry. Bring to a boil, then add shrimp, scallops and mussels. Simmer covered 3 minutes or until seafood is done and mussel shells open. (Discard any unopened shells.) Stir in cream blended with flour and cook over medium heat, stirring occasionally, 2 minutes or until sauce is slightly thickened. Stir in salt and pepper. Serve over hot pasta and sprinkle, if desired, with freshly ground pepper and grated Parmesan cheese.

*Also terrific with WISH-BONE® Robusto Italian, Italian & Cheese, Herbal Italian, Blended Italian, Classic Dijon Vinaigrette, Olive Oil Vinaigrette or Lite Classic Dijon Vinaigrette Dressing.

Easy Beef Stroganoff

Makes about 2 servings

2 tablespoons oil
2 teaspoons finely chopped garlic
1/2 pound boneless sirloin steak, cut into thin strips
1/4 cup dry red wine
2 teaspoons Worcestershire sauce
1 1/4 cups water
1/2 cup milk
2 tablespoons butter or margarine
1 package **LIPTON®** Noodles & Sauce– Stroganoff*
1/2 cup pearl onions

In large skillet, heat oil and cook garlic over medium heat 30 seconds. Add beef and cook over medium-high heat 1 minute or until almost done. Add wine and Worcestershire sauce and cook 30 seconds; remove beef. Into skillet, stir water, milk, butter and noodles & stroganoff sauce. Bring to the boiling point, then continue boiling, stirring occasionally, 7 minutes. Stir in onions and beef, then cook 2 minutes or until noodles are tender. Garnish, if desired, with chopped parsley and paprika.

Also terrific with LIPTON® Noodles & Sauce—Beef Flavor.

Land O Lakes® Chicken Kiev

Makes 4 servings

Filling
- 1/3 cup chopped fresh mushrooms
- 1/4 cup LAND O LAKES® Unsalted Butter, softened
- 1 (2-oz.) jar diced pimiento, drained
- 1 tablespoon chopped green onion
- 1/4 teaspoon salt
- 1/8 teaspoon pepper

Chicken
- 4 whole boneless chicken breasts, skinned
- 1/4 cup LAND O LAKES® Unsalted Butter
- 1/2 cup fine, dry bread crumbs
- 1/4 teaspoon dried thyme leaves
- 1/4 teaspoon dried rubbed sage

Stir together all filling ingredients in medium bowl. Divide into 4 equal portions. Freeze portions for 30 minutes or longer. *Heat oven to 350°F.* Flatten each chicken breast to about 1/4-inch thickness by pounding between sheets of waxed paper. Place portion of frozen filling onto each flattened chicken breast. Roll and tuck in edges of chicken breast; fasten with skewer or wooden picks. In 12×8-inch baking pan melt 1/4 cup butter in oven (4 to 6 minutes). Combine bread crumbs, thyme and sage. Dip rolled chicken breasts in melted butter, then coat with crumbs. Place chicken breasts in same baking pan; sprinkle with remaining crumbs. Bake for 55 to 65 minutes or until chicken breasts are fork tender. Remove skewers before serving. To serve, spoon butter over chicken breasts.

Roast Stuffed Turkey

Roast Stuffed Turkey

Makes 8 to 10 servings

- 2 packages (6 oz. each) STOVE TOP® Stuffing Mix, any variety
- 1/2 cup (1 stick) butter or margarine, cut into pieces
- 3 cups hot water
- 1 (8- to 10-pound) turkey

Prepare stuffing by placing contents of vegetable/seasoning packets and butter in a large bowl. Add hot water; stir just to partially melt butter. Add stuffing crumbs. Stir just to moisten. *Do not stuff bird until ready to roast.*

Rinse turkey with cold water; pat dry. *Do not* rub cavity with salt. Lightly stuff neck and body cavities with prepared stuffing. Skewer neck skin to back. Tie legs to tail and twist wing tips under. Place turkey breast side up in roasting pan. Roast at 325°F for 3 to 4 hours or as directed on poultry wrapper. Bake any remaining stuffing at 325°F for 30 minutes. Cover the baking dish for moist stuffing. If drier stuffing is desired, bake uncovered.

Cookies & Candies

Lemon Nut Bars

Makes about 3 dozen

1 1/3 cups flour
1/2 cup packed brown sugar
1/4 cup granulated sugar
3/4 cup PARKAY® Margarine
1 cup old fashioned or quick oats, uncooked
1/2 cup chopped nuts
1 8-oz. pkg. PHILADELPHIA BRAND® Cream Cheese, softened
1 egg
3 tablespoons lemon juice
1 tablespoon grated lemon peel

Preheat oven to 350°F. Stir together flour and sugars in medium bowl. Cut in margarine until mixture resembles coarse crumbs. Stir in oats and nuts. Reserve 1 cup crumb mixture; press remaining crumb mixture onto bottom of greased 13×9-inch baking pan. Bake 15 minutes. Beat cream cheese, egg, juice and peel in small mixing bowl at medium speed with electric mixer until well blended. Pour over crust; sprinkle with reserved crumb mixture. Bake 25 minutes. Cool; cut into bars.

Preparation time: 30 minutes
Cooking time: 25 minutes

Chocolate Sugar Cookies

Makes about 3 1/2 dozen

3 squares BAKER'S® Unsweetened Chocolate
1 cup (2 sticks) butter or margarine
1 cup sugar
1 egg
1 teaspoon vanilla
2 cups all-purpose flour
1 teaspoon baking soda
1/4 teaspoon salt
Additional granulated sugar

Microwave chocolate and butter in large microwavable bowl at HIGH 2 minutes or until butter is melted. *Stir until chocolate is completely melted.* Stir 1 cup sugar into melted chocolate until well blended. Stir in egg and vanilla until completely mixed. Mix in flour, baking soda and salt until well blended. Chill dough until easy to handle, about 30 minutes. Shape into 1-inch balls; roll in sugar. Place on greased cookie sheet. (If a flatter, crisper cookie is desired, flatten with bottom of glass.) Bake at 375°F for 8 to 10 minutes or until set. Remove and cool on rack.

Range Top: Melt chocolate and butter in heavy saucepan over very low heat; stir constantly until just melted. Remove from heat; continue as directed above.

Kahlúa® Kisses (left), Kahlúa® Bonbons (right)

Kahlúa® Bonbons

Makes 4 dozen

¼ cup **KAHLÚA®**
4 teaspoons instant coffee powder
¾ cup unsalted butter, softened
1 ounce cream cheese, softened
2 egg yolks
1½ cups powdered sugar
12 ounces semisweet chocolate, chopped
¼ cup vegetable shortening
10 ounces amaretti cookies*, crushed

In small bowl combine KAHLÚA® and coffee powder. Let stand 10 minutes. In medium bowl, cream butter with cream cheese until fluffy. Add egg yolks and sugar and beat until smooth. Stir KAHLÚA® and coffee powder until powder is completely dissolved. Gradually beat into butter mixture. Drop mixture by rounded teaspoonfuls onto baking sheets or trays lined with waxed paper or plastic wrap. Set in freezer 1 hour or overnight.

When ready to dip, remove from freezer 1 sheet at a time; roll between palms to shape into balls. Return to freezer.

Melt chocolate and shortening in top of double boiler over simmering water, stirring frequently. Cool to lukewarm, stirring occasionally. Place crushed amaretti in bowl.

Using wooden skewer or toothpick, dip bonbon balls, 1 at a time, into warm chocolate. Allow excess chocolate to drip off, then transfer to bowl of amaretti crumbs. Using small spoon, sprinkle crumbs over bonbon to cover completely. Transfer to baking sheets or trays lined with clean plastic wrap. Using second skewer, gently push bonbon off dipping skewer. If hole remains, cover with additional amaretti crumbs. If chocolate becomes too thick, reheat gently as needed. Store bonbons in refrigerator.

*Amaretti are Italian meringue cookies and can be purchased at Italian or specialty food shops. If desired, substitute an equal amount of finely chopped toasted hazelnuts or almonds.

Kahlúa® Kisses

Makes 2½ dozen

¾ teaspoon instant coffee powder
⅓ cup water
1 cup plus 2 tablespoons sugar
¼ cup KAHLÚA®
3 egg whites, room temperature
¼ teaspoon cream of tartar
Dash salt

In heavy 2-quart saucepan, dissolve coffee powder in water. Add 1 cup sugar; stir over low heat until sugar dissolves. Do not allow to boil. Stir in KAHLÚA®. Brush down sides of pan with pastry brush dipped frequently into cold water. Bring mixture to a boil over medium heat. *Do not stir.* Boil until candy thermometer registers 240° to 242°F, about 15 minutes, adjusting heat if necessary to prevent boiling over. Mixture will be very thick. Remove from heat (temperature will continue to rise).

Immediately beat egg whites with cream of tartar and salt until soft peaks form. Add remaining 2 tablespoons sugar; continue beating until stiff peaks form. Gradually beat hot KAHLÚA® syrup into egg whites, beating after each addition to thoroughly mix. Continue beating 4 to 5 minutes or until meringue is very thick, firm and cooled to lukewarm.

Line baking sheet with foil, shiny side down. Using pastry bag fitted with large (#6) star tip, pipe meringue into kisses about 1½ inches wide at base and 1½ inches high onto baking sheet. Set on center rack of 200°F oven for 4 hours. Without opening door, turn heat off and let kisses dry in oven 2 more hours or until crisp. Remove from oven; cool completely on pan. Store in airtight container up to 1 week.

Snowballs

Makes 5 dozen cookies

½ cup DOMINO® Confectioners 10-X Sugar
¼ teaspoon salt
1 cup butter or margarine, softened
1 teaspoon vanilla extract
2¼ cups all-purpose flour
½ cup chopped pecans
DOMINO® Confectioners 10-X Sugar

In large bowl, combine ½ cup sugar, salt and butter; mix well. Add extract. Gradually stir in flour. Work nuts into dough. Chill well. Form into 1-inch balls. Place on ungreased cookie sheets. Bake at 400°F for 8 to 10 minutes or until set but not brown. Roll in confectioners sugar immediately. Cool on rack. Roll in sugar again. Store in airtight container.

Lemon Cut-Out Cookies

Makes 4 to 5 dozen

2¾ cups unsifted flour
1 teaspoon baking powder
½ teaspoon baking soda
¼ teaspoon salt
½ cup margarine or butter, softened
1½ cups sugar
1 egg
⅓ cup REALEMON® Lemon Juice from Concentrate
Lemon Icing, optional

Stir together flour, baking powder, baking soda and salt; set aside. In large mixer bowl, beat margarine and sugar until fluffy; beat in egg. Gradually add dry ingredients alternately with REALEMON® brand; mix well (dough will be soft). Chill overnight in refrigerator or 2 hours in freezer. Preheat oven to 375°F. On well-floured surface, roll out one-third of dough to ⅛-inch thickness; cut with floured cookie cutters. Place 1 inch apart on greased baking sheets; bake 8 to 10 minutes. Cool. Repeat with remaining dough. Ice and decorate as desired.

Lemon Icing: Mix 1¼ cups confectioners' sugar and 2 tablespoons REALEMON® brand until smooth. Add food coloring if desired. Makes about ½ cup.

Lemon Cut-Out Cookies

Chocolate Almond Buttons

Makes 6 dozen cookies

1 1/3 cups flour
1/3 cup unsweetened cocoa powder
1/4 teaspoon salt
1 cup **BLUE DIAMOND®** Blanched Almond
   Paste
1/2 cup plus 1 1/2 tablespoons softened butter,
   divided
1/4 cup corn syrup
1 teaspoon vanilla extract
3 squares (1 ounce each) semisweet chocolate
2/3 cup **BLUE DIAMOND®** Blanched Whole
   Almonds, toasted

Sift flour, cocoa powder, and salt; reserve. Cream almond paste and 1/2 cup butter until smooth. Beat in corn syrup and vanilla. Beat in flour mixture, scraping sides of bowl occasionally, until well-blended. Shape into 3/4-inch balls. Place on lightly greased cookie sheet; indent center of cookies with finger. Bake at 350°F for 8 to 10 minutes or until done. (Cookies will be soft but will become firm when cooled.) In top of double boiler, stir chocolate and remaining 1 1/2 tablespoons butter over simmering water until melted and smooth. With spoon, drizzle small amount of chocolate into center of each cookie. Press an almond into chocolate on each cookie.

Chocolate Almond Buttons

Peanut Butter Kisses

Makes 6 to 7 1/2 dozen cookies

1 cup **BUTTER FLAVOR CRISCO®**
1 cup **JIF®** Creamy Peanut Butter
1 cup firmly packed brown sugar
1 cup granulated sugar
2 eggs
1/4 cup milk
2 teaspoons vanilla
3 1/4 cups all-purpose flour
2 teaspoons baking soda
1 teaspoon salt
   Granulated sugar for rolling
72 to 90 milk chocolate kisses or stars,
   unwrapped

Heat oven to 375°F. Combine BUTTER FLAVOR CRISCO®, JIF® Creamy Peanut Butter, brown sugar and 1 cup granulated sugar in large bowl. Beat at medium speed of electric mixer until well blended. Beat in eggs, milk and vanilla. Combine flour, baking soda and salt. Mix into creamed mixture at low speed until just blended. Dough will be stiff.

Form dough into 1-inch balls. Roll in granulated sugar. Place 2 inches apart on ungreased baking sheet. Bake for 8 minutes. Press milk chocolate kiss into center of each cookie. Return to oven. Bake 3 minutes. Cool 2 minutes on baking sheet. Remove to cooling rack.

Jam-Filled Peanut Butter Kisses: Omit milk chocolate kisses. Prepare recipe as directed through placing balls on baking sheet. Bake at 375°F for 8 minutes. Press handle of wooden spoon gently in center of each cookie. Return to oven. Bake 3 minutes. Finish as directed. Fill cooled cookies with favorite jam.

Austrian Tea Cookies

Makes 3 1/2 dozen

1 1/2 cups sugar, divided
1/2 cup butter, softened
1/2 cup vegetable shortening
1 egg, beaten
1/2 teaspoon vanilla extract
2 cups all-purpose flour
2 cups **ALMOND DELIGHT®** brand cereal,
   crushed to 1 cup
1/2 teaspoon baking powder
1/4 teaspoon ground cinnamon
14 ounces almond paste
2 egg whites
5 tablespoons raspberry or apricot jam, warmed

In large bowl beat 1 cup sugar, the butter and shortening. Add egg and vanilla; mix well. Stir in flour, cereal, baking powder and cinnamon until well combined. Chill 1 to 2 hours or until firm.

Preheat oven to 350°F. Roll dough on lightly floured surface to ¼-inch thickness; cut into 2-inch circles. Place on ungreased cookie sheet; set aside. In small bowl beat almond paste, egg whites and remaining ½ cup sugar until smooth. With pastry tube fitted with medium-sized star tip, pipe almond paste mixture ½-inch thick on top of each cookie along outside edge. Place ¼ teaspoon jam in center of cookie, spreading out to paste. Bake 8 to 10 minutes or until lightly browned. Let stand 1 minute before removing from sheet. Cool on wire rack.

Disco Whirls

Makes about 3½ dozen cookies

½ cup butter or margarine, softened
¾ cup granulated sugar
1 egg
1 teaspoon vanilla
1½ cups all-purpose flour
¼ teaspoon baking powder
3 tablespoons packed brown sugar
1½ teaspoons unsweetened cocoa powder
2 teaspoons milk
¾ cup DIAMOND® Walnuts, finely chopped

In medium bowl, beat butter, granulated sugar, egg and vanilla. In small bowl, sift flour with baking powder. Blend into creamed mixture to make a stiff dough. Cover and chill dough about 1 hour for easier handling. In small bowl, mix brown sugar, cocoa and milk; set aside. Roll out dough on lightly floured pastry cloth or board into 10-inch square. Spread with cocoa mixture and sprinkle with walnuts, leaving about ½ inch uncovered at opposite sides of dough. Roll up tightly, jelly-roll fashion, starting at 1 side where dough is not spread with filling. Wrap in plastic wrap and freeze until firm, several hours or overnight. Cut into ¼-inch slices and arrange on lightly greased cookie sheets. Bake in preheated 375°F oven 14 to 15 minutes or until edges are lightly browned. Remove to wire racks to cool.

Almond Butter Crunch

Almond Butter Crunch

Makes about ¾ pound

1 cup BLUE DIAMOND® Blanched Slivered Almonds
½ cup butter
½ cup sugar
1 tablespoon light corn syrup

Line bottom and sides of an 8- or 9-inch cake pan with aluminum foil (*not* plastic wrap or wax paper). Butter foil heavily; reserve. Combine almonds, butter, sugar, and corn syrup in 10-inch skillet. Bring to a boil over medium heat, stirring constantly. Boil, stirring constantly, until mixture turns golden brown, about 5 to 6 minutes. Working quickly, spread candy in prepared pan. Cool about 15 minutes or until firm. Remove candy from pan by lifting edges of foil. Peel off foil. Cool thoroughly. Break into pieces.

Triple Chocolate Squares

Triple Chocolate Squares

Makes 64 squares

1½ cups **BLUE DIAMOND®** Blanched Almond
   Paste, divided
  8 ounces semisweet chocolate, melted
 ¾ cup softened butter, divided
  8 ounces milk chocolate, melted
  8 ounces white chocolate, melted

Line bottom and sides of 8-inch square pan with
aluminum foil. Beat ½ cup almond paste with
semisweet chocolate. Beat in ¼ cup butter. Spread
evenly in bottom of prepared pan. Chill to harden.
Beat ½ cup almond paste with milk chocolate. Beat
in ¼ cup butter. Spread mixture evenly over chilled
semisweet chocolate layer. Chill to harden. Beat
remaining ½ cup almond paste with white chocolate.
Beat in remaining ¼ cup butter. Spread mixture
evenly over milk chocolate layer. Chill. Remove
candy from pan by lifting edges of foil. Peel off foil
and cut candy into 1-inch squares.

Sparkly Cookie Stars

Makes about 6½ dozen 3-inch cookies

3½ cups unsifted flour
  1 tablespoon baking powder
 ½ teaspoon salt
  1 (14-ounce) can **EAGLE®** Brand Sweetened
    Condensed Milk (NOT evaporated milk)
 ¾ cup margarine or butter, softened
  2 eggs
  1 tablespoon vanilla *or* 2 teaspoons almond or
    lemon extract
  1 egg white, slightly beaten
    Red and green colored sugars *or* colored
    sprinkles

Combine flour, baking powder and salt. In large
mixer bowl, beat sweetened condensed milk,
margarine, eggs and vanilla until well blended. Add
dry ingredients; mix well. Chill 2 hours. On floured
surface, knead dough to form a smooth ball. Divide
into thirds. On well-floured surface, roll out each
portion to ⅛-inch thickness. Cut with floured star
cookie cutter. Reroll as necessary to use all dough.
Place 1 inch apart on greased baking sheets. Brush
with egg white; sprinkle with sugar. Bake in
preheated 350°F oven 7 to 9 minutes or until lightly
browned around edges *(do not overbake)*. Cool. Store
loosely covered at room temperature.

Note: *If desired, cut small stars from dough and place on top
of larger stars. Proceed as above.*

Chocolate Mint Truffles

Makes about 6 dozen

1 (10-ounce) package mint chocolate chips
1 (6-ounce) package semi-sweet chocolate chips
  (1 cup)
1 (14-ounce) can **EAGLE®** Brand Sweetened
  Condensed Milk (NOT evaporated milk)
  Finely chopped nuts, flaked coconut,
    chocolate sprinkles, colored sprinkles,
    unsweetened cocoa *or* colored sugar

In heavy saucepan, over low heat, melt chips with
sweetened condensed milk. Chill 2 hours or until
firm. Shape into 1-inch balls; roll in any of the above
coatings. Chill 1 hour or until firm. Store covered at
room temperature.

Microwave: In 1-quart glass measure, combine chips
and sweetened condensed milk. Cook on 100%
power (high) 3 minutes or until chips melt, stirring
after each 1½ minutes. Stir until smooth. Proceed as
above.

Black Forest Brownies

Makes 24 to 36 brownies

1 (12-ounce) package semi-sweet chocolate chips
¼ cup margarine or butter
2 cups biscuit baking mix
1 (14-ounce) can EAGLE® Brand Sweetened
    Condensed Milk (NOT evaporated milk)
1 egg, beaten
1 teaspoon almond extract
½ cup chopped candied cherries
½ cup sliced almonds, toasted

Preheat oven to 350°F. In large saucepan, over low heat, melt *1 cup* chips with margarine; remove from heat. Add biscuit mix, sweetened condensed milk, egg and extract. Stir in remaining chips and cherries. Turn into well-greased 13×9-inch baking pan. Top with almonds. Bake 20 to 25 minutes or until brownies begin to pull away from sides of pan. Cool. Cut into bars. Store tightly covered at room temperature.

Sparkly Cookie Stars (top left), Black Forest Brownies (top right), Chocolate Mint Truffles (bottom)

Fruit Burst Cookies

Makes 2½ dozen

1 cup margarine or butter, softened
¼ cup sugar
1 teaspoon almond extract
2 cups all-purpose flour
½ teaspoon salt
1 cup finely chopped nuts
    SMUCKER'S® Simply Fruit

Cream margarine and sugar until light and fluffy. Blend in almond extract. Combine flour and salt; add to mixture and blend well. Shape level tablespoons of dough into balls; roll in nuts. Place 2 inches apart on ungreased cookie sheets; flatten slightly. Indent centers; fill with fruit spread. Bake at 400°F for 10 to 12 minutes or just until lightly browned. Cool.

Walnut Jam Crescents

Makes 2 dozen crescents

⅔ cup butter or margarine
1⅓ cups all-purpose flour
½ cup dairy sour cream
⅔ cup raspberry jam or orange marmalade
⅔ cup DIAMOND® Walnuts, finely chopped

In medium bowl, cut butter into flour until mixture resembles fine crumbs. Add sour cream and mix until stiff dough is formed. Divide evenly into 2 portions. Shape each into a ball, flatten slightly, wrap in waxed paper and chill well. Working with 1 portion of dough at a time, roll dough into 11-inch round on lightly floured pastry cloth or board. Spread with ⅓ cup of the jam and sprinkle with ⅓ cup of the walnuts. Cut into quarters, then cut each quarter into 3 wedges. Roll up, 1 at a time, starting from outer edge, and place on lightly greased cookie sheets. Repeat with second portion of dough. Bake in preheated 375°F oven 25 to 30 minutes or until lightly browned. Remove to wire racks to cool.

Apricot Almond Chewies

Makes about 6½ dozen

4 cups finely chopped dried apricots (about
  1 pound)
4 cups flaked coconut *or* coconut macaroon
  crumbs (about 21 macaroons)
2 cups slivered almonds, toasted and finely
  chopped
1 (14-ounce) can EAGLE® Brand Sweetened
  Condensed Milk (NOT evaporated milk)
  Whole almonds, optional

In large bowl, combine all ingredients except whole
almonds. Chill 2 hours. Shape into 1-inch balls. Top
each with whole almond if desired. Store tightly
covered in refrigerator.

Chipper Peanut Candy

Makes about 2 pounds

1 (6-ounce) package semi-sweet chocolate chips
  (1 cup) *or* butterscotch flavored chips
1 (14-ounce) can EAGLE® Brand Sweetened
  Condensed Milk (NOT evaporated milk)
1 cup peanut butter
2 cups crushed potato chips
1 cup coarsely chopped peanuts

In large heavy saucepan, over low heat, melt
chocolate chips with sweetened condensed milk and
peanut butter; stir until well blended. Remove from
heat. Add potato chips and peanuts; mix well. Press
into aluminum foil-lined 8- or 9-inch square pan.
Chill 2 hours or until firm. Turn onto cutting board;
peel off foil and cut into squares. Store loosely
covered at room temperature.

Microwave: In 2-quart glass measure, combine
chocolate chips, sweetened condensed milk and
peanut butter. Cook on 100% power (high) 4
minutes, stirring after each 2 minutes. Proceed as
above.

Caramel Peanut Balls

Makes about 4½ dozen

3 cups finely chopped dry roasted peanuts
1 (14-ounce) can EAGLE® Brand Sweetened
  Condensed Milk (NOT evaporated milk)
1 teaspoon vanilla extract
½ pound chocolate confectioners' coating*

In heavy saucepan, combine peanuts, sweetened
condensed milk and vanilla. Over medium heat, cook
and stir 8 to 10 minutes or until mixture forms ball
around spoon and pulls away from side of pan. Cool
10 minutes. Chill if desired. Shape into 1-inch balls.
In small heavy saucepan, over low heat, melt
confectioners' coating. With wooden pick, dip each
ball into melted coating, covering half of ball. Place
on wax paper-lined baking sheets until firm. Store
covered at room temperature or in refrigerator.

**Chocolate confectioners' coating can be purchased in candy
specialty stores.*

Crunchy Clusters

Makes about 3 dozen

1 (12-ounce) package semi-sweet chocolate chips
  or 3 (6-ounce) packages butterscotch
  flavored chips
1 (14-ounce) can EAGLE® Brand Sweetened
  Condensed Milk (NOT evaporated milk)
1 (3-ounce) can chow mein noodles *or* 2 cups
  pretzel sticks, broken into ½-inch pieces
1 cup dry roasted peanuts *or* whole roasted
  almonds

In heavy saucepan, over low heat, melt chips with
sweetened condensed milk. Remove from heat. In
large bowl, combine noodles and nuts; stir in
chocolate mixture. Drop by tablespoonfuls onto wax
paper-lined baking sheets; chill 2 hours or until firm.
Store loosely covered at room temperature.

Microwave: In 2-quart glass measure, combine chips
and sweetened condensed milk. Cook on 100%
power (high) 3 minutes, stirring after each 1½
minutes. Stir until smooth. Proceed as above.

*Top to bottom: Apricot Almond Chewies,
Chipper Peanut Candy, Caramel Peanut Balls,
Crunchy Clusters—Butterscotch and Chocolate,
Chipper Peanut Candy*

Jam-Up Oatmeal Cookies

Jam-Up Oatmeal Cookies

Makes about 2 dozen cookies

1 cup **BUTTER FLAVOR CRISCO®**
1 1/2 cups firmly packed brown sugar
2 eggs
2 teaspoons almond extract
2 cups all-purpose flour
1 teaspoon baking powder
1 teaspoon salt
1/2 teaspoon baking soda
2 1/2 cups quick oats (not instant or old fashioned)
1 cup finely chopped pecans
1 jar (12 ounces) pineapple jam
Granulated sugar for sprinkling

Combine BUTTER FLAVOR CRISCO® and sugar in large bowl. Beat at medium speed of electric mixer until well blended. Beat in eggs and almond extract. Combine flour, baking powder, salt and baking soda. Mix into creamed mixture at low speed until just blended. Stir in oats and chopped nuts with spoon. Cover and refrigerate at least 1 hour.

Heat oven to 350°F. Grease baking sheet with BUTTER FLAVOR CRISCO®. Roll out 1/2 of the dough, at a time, to about 1/4-inch thickness on floured surface. Cut out with 2 1/2-inch round cookie cutter. Place 1 teaspoonful of jam in center of 1/2 of the rounds. Top with remaining rounds. Press edges to seal. Prick center. Sprinkle with sugar. Place 1 inch apart on baking sheet. Bake for 12 to 15 minutes, or until lightly browned. Cool 2 minutes on baking sheet. Remove to cooling rack.

Cut-Out Sugar Cookies

Makes about 3 dozen cookies

2/3 cup **BUTTER FLAVOR CRISCO®**
3/4 cup sugar
1 tablespoon plus 1 teaspoon milk
1 teaspoon vanilla
1 egg
2 cups all-purpose flour
1 1/2 teaspoons baking powder
1/4 teaspoon salt

Combine BUTTER FLAVOR CRISCO®, sugar, milk and vanilla in large bowl. Beat at medium speed of electric mixer until well blended. Beat in egg. Combine flour, baking powder and salt. Mix into creamed mixture at low speed until well blended. Cover and refrigerate several hours or overnight.

Heat oven to 375°F. Roll out 1/2 of the dough, at a time, to about 1/8-inch thickness on floured surface. Cut out with cookie cutters. Place 2 inches apart on ungreased baking sheet. Sprinkle with colored sugars and decors or leave plain and frost* when cooled. Bake for 7 to 9 minutes, or until set. Remove immediately to cooling rack.

Lemon or Orange Cut-Out Sugar Cookies: Add 1 teaspoon grated lemon or orange peel and 1 teaspoon lemon or orange extract to dough before flour is added.

Creamy Vanilla Frosting: Combine 1/2 cup BUTTER FLAVOR CRISCO®, 1 pound (4 cups) powdered sugar, 1/3 cup milk and 1 teaspoon vanilla in medium bowl. Beat at low speed of electric mixer until well blended. Scrape bowl. Beat at high speed for 2 minutes, or until smooth and creamy. One or two drops food color can be used to tint each cup of frosting, if desired. Frost cooled cookies. This frosting works well in decorating tube.

Lemon or Orange Creamy Frosting: Omit milk. Add 1/3 cup lemon or orange juice. Add 1 teaspoon orange peel with orange juice.

Walnut Shortbread Bars

Makes about 5 dozen

1 8-oz. pkg. PHILADELPHIA BRAND® Cream
  Cheese, softened
1 cup PARKAY® Margarine
¾ cup granulated sugar
¾ cup packed brown sugar
1 egg
1 teaspoon vanilla
2½ cups flour
1 teaspoon CALUMET® Baking Powder
½ teaspoon salt
¾ cup chopped walnuts

Preheat oven to 350°F. Beat cream cheese, margarine
and sugars in large mixing bowl at medium speed
with electric mixer until well blended. Blend in egg
and vanilla. Add combined dry ingredients; mix
well. Stir in walnuts. Spread into greased 15×10×1-
inch jelly roll pan. Bake 20 to 25 minutes or until
lightly browned. Cool. Sprinkle with powdered
sugar, if desired. Cut into bars.

Preparation time: 15 minutes
Cooking time: 25 minutes

Chocolate Peanut Butter Balls

Makes 4½ dozen

1 cup crunchy peanut butter
¼ cup margarine or butter, softened
2 cups KELLOGG'S® RICE KRISPIES® cereal
1 cup confectioners sugar
1 package (14 oz.) chocolate candy coating
2 tablespoons shortening
  White candy coating, melted (optional)

In large bowl, combine peanut butter and margarine.
Add KELLOGG'S® RICE KRISPIES® cereal and
sugar, mixing until evenly combined. Portion cereal
mixture, using a rounded measuring-teaspoon. Roll
into balls; set aside.

In top of double boiler, over hot water, melt
chocolate coating and shortening. Dip each peanut
butter ball in coating and place on waxed paper-lined
baking sheet. Drizzle with melted white coating, if
desired. Refrigerate until firm. Place in small candy
paper cups to serve.

*Note: One package (12 oz.) semi-sweet chocolate morsels may
be used in place of chocolate candy coating.*

Per Serving (1 ball): 90 Calories

Crisp Chocolate Truffles

Makes 4½ dozen

1 jar (7 oz.) marshmallow creme
2 tablespoons margarine or butter
1 package (6 oz.) semi-sweet chocolate morsels
  (1 cup)
2 cups KELLOGG'S® RICE KRISPIES® cereal
1 package (14 oz.) white candy coating
2 tablespoons shortening
  Multicolored sprinkles (optional)

In heavy 2-quart saucepan, combine marshmallow
creme, margarine and chocolate morsels. Cook over
low heat, stirring constantly, until chocolate is melted
and mixture is smooth; remove from heat. Stir
KELLOGG'S® RICE KRISPIES® cereal into hot
chocolate mixture, mixing until thoroughly
combined. Drop by rounded measuring-teaspoonfuls
onto waxed paper-lined baking sheet. Refrigerate
until firm, about 1 hour.

In top of double boiler, over hot water, melt white
coating and shortening. Dip each chocolate ball in
coating and place on waxed paper-lined baking sheet.
Decorate with sprinkles, if desired. Refrigerate until
firm. Place in small candy paper cups to serve.

Per Serving (1 truffle): 80 Calories

Chocolate Peanut Butter Balls, Crisp Chocolate Truffles

Pecan Pie Bars

Makes 36 bars

2 cups unsifted flour
1/2 cup confectioners' sugar
1 cup cold margarine or butter
1 (14-ounce) can EAGLE® Brand Sweetened
    Condensed Milk (NOT evaporated milk)
1 egg
1 teaspoon vanilla extract
1 (6-ounce) package almond brickle chips
1 cup chopped pecans

Preheat oven to 350°F (325° for glass dish). In medium bowl, combine flour and sugar; cut in margarine until crumbly. Press firmly on bottom of 13×9-inch baking pan. Bake 15 minutes. Meanwhile, in medium bowl, beat sweetened condensed milk, egg and vanilla. Stir in chips and pecans. Spread evenly over crust. Bake 25 minutes or until golden brown. Cool. Cut into bars. Store covered in refrigerator.

Triple Layer Cookie Bars

Makes 24 to 36 bars

1/2 cup margarine or butter
1 1/2 cups graham cracker crumbs
1 (7-ounce) package flaked coconut (2 2/3 cups)
1 (14-ounce) can EAGLE® Brand Sweetened
    Condensed Milk (NOT evaporated milk)
1 (12-ounce) package semi-sweet chocolate chips
1/2 cup creamy peanut butter

Preheat oven to 350°F (325° for glass dish). In 13×9-inch baking pan, melt margarine in oven. Sprinkle crumbs evenly over margarine. Top evenly with coconut then sweetened condensed milk. Bake 25 minutes or until lightly browned. In small saucepan, over low heat, melt chips with peanut butter. Spread evenly over hot coconut layer. Cool 30 minutes. Chill thoroughly. Cut into bars. Garnish as desired. Store loosely covered at room temperature.

Meringue Kisses

Makes 4 to 5 dozen cookies

2 egg whites
1/4 teaspoon cream of tartar
1/2 cup sugar
    Variation Ingredients* (optional)

In small mixer bowl, beat egg whites with cream of tartar at high speed until foamy. Add sugar, 2 tablespoons at a time, beating constantly until sugar is dissolved and whites are glossy and stand in stiff peaks. If desired, beat or fold in Variation Ingredients. Drop meringue by rounded teaspoonfuls or pipe through pastry tube 1 inch apart onto greased or waxed-paper-lined cookie sheets. Bake in preheated 225°F oven until firm, about 1 hour. Turn off oven. Let cookies stand in oven with door closed until cool, dry and crisp, at least 1 additional hour. Store in tightly sealed container.

Variation Ingredients: Amounts listed are for one batch of cookies. To make two variations at a time, divide meringue mixture equally between two bowls. Beat or fold into each bowl half of the amounts listed for each variation.

Chocolate: Beat in 1/4 cup unsweetened cocoa and 1 teaspoon vanilla.

Citrus: Beat in 1 tablespoon grated orange peel, 1/4 teaspoon lemon extract and a few drops yellow food coloring.

Mint: Beat in 1/4 teaspoon mint extract and a few drops green food coloring.

Rocky Road: Beat in 1 teaspoon vanilla. Fold in 1/2 cup semisweet chocolate chips and 1/2 cup chopped nuts.

Cherry-Almond: Fold in 1/2 cup chopped, drained maraschino cherries and 1/2 cup chopped almonds.

Favorite recipe from **American Egg Board**

Pecan Pie Bars (left), Triple Layer Cookie Bars (right)

Simply Delicious Minty Cookies

Makes about 5 dozen cookies

1 cup BUTTER FLAVOR CRISCO®
1 package (8 ounces) cream cheese, softened
³/₄ cup granulated sugar
¹/₂ cup firmly packed brown sugar
1 teaspoon vanilla
2 cups all-purpose flour
1³/₄ cups mint chocolate chips

Heat oven to 350°F. Combine BUTTER FLAVOR CRISCO®, cream cheese, granulated sugar, brown sugar and vanilla in large bowl. Beat at medium speed of electric mixer until well blended. Mix flour into creamed mixture at low speed until just blended. Stir in mint chocolate chips. Drop rounded teaspoonfuls of dough 2 inches apart onto ungreased baking sheet. Bake for 8 minutes, or until lightly browned. Cool 2 minutes on baking sheet. Remove to cooling rack.

Kris Kringle Cookies (top), Lebkuchen Jewels (bottom)

Lebkuchen Jewels

Makes about 4 dozen cookies

³/₄ cup packed brown sugar
1 egg
1 cup honey
1 tablespoon grated lemon peel
1 teaspoon lemon juice
2³/₄ cups all-purpose flour
1 teaspoon *each* ground nutmeg, cinnamon and cloves
¹/₂ teaspoon *each* baking soda and salt
1 cup SUN-MAID® Golden Raisins
¹/₂ cup *each* mixed candied fruits and citron
1 cup chopped DIAMOND® Walnuts
Lemon Glaze (recipe follows)
Candied cherries and citron, for garnish

In large bowl, beat sugar and egg until smooth and fluffy. Add honey, lemon peel and juice; beat well. In medium bowl, sift flour with nutmeg, cinnamon, cloves, baking soda and salt; gradually mix into egg-sugar mixture on low speed. Stir in fruits and nuts. Spread batter into greased 15×10-inch jelly-roll pan. Bake in preheated 375°F oven 20 minutes or until lightly browned. Cool slightly in pan; brush with Lemon Glaze. Cool; cut into diamonds. Decorate with candied cherries and slivers of citron, if desired. Store in covered container up to 1 month.

Lemon Glaze: In small bowl, combine 1 cup sifted powdered sugar with enough lemon juice (1¹/₂ to 2 tablespoons) to make a thin glaze.

Kris Kringle Cookies

Makes 1¹/₂ to 2 dozen cookies

1¹/₃ cups butter or margarine, softened
1¹/₃ cups granulated sugar
2 eggs
2²/₃ cups all-purpose flour
¹/₄ teaspoon salt
1¹/₂ cups SUN-MAID® Raisins, chopped
¹/₂ cup chopped candied ginger*
1 egg white, beaten for glaze
Colored sugars, dragées, candied fruits and DIAMOND® Walnuts, for garnish

In large bowl, cream butter, granulated sugar and eggs. Stir in flour and salt, mixing until blended. Stir in raisins and ginger. Cover and chill dough. Roll out dough on lightly floured board to ¹/₈-inch thickness; cut into desired shapes with sharp-edged cookie cutters. Space 2 inches apart on greased baking sheets. Brush with beaten white; sprinkle with additional granulated sugar, or decorate with colored sugars, dragées, candied fruits and walnuts, if desired. Bake in preheated 350°F oven 12 to 15 minutes or until golden. Cool 2 to 3 minutes on pan; remove to wire rack to cool completely.

**An additional ¹/₂ cup of raisins may be substituted for candied ginger; add 1 tablespoon ground ginger.*

One-Bowl Homemade Brownies from Baker's®

One-Bowl Homemade Brownies from Baker's®

Makes 24 brownies

4 squares BAKER'S® Unsweetened Chocolate
¾ cup (1½ sticks) margarine or butter
2 cups sugar
3 eggs
1 teaspoon vanilla
1 cup all-purpose flour
1 cup coarsely chopped nuts (optional)

Microwave chocolate and margarine in large microwavable bowl at HIGH 2 minutes or until margarine is melted. *Stir until chocolate is completely melted.* Stir in sugar until well blended. Stir in eggs and vanilla until completely mixed. Mix in flour until well blended. Stir in nuts. Spread in greased 13×9-inch pan. Bake at 350°F for 35 to 40 minutes or until wooden pick inserted into center comes out almost clean. *(Do not overbake.)* Cool in pan; cut into squares.

Range Top: Melt chocolate and margarine in 3-quart saucepan over very low heat; stir constantly until just melted. Remove from heat. Continue as above.

Brownie Options

Cakelike Brownies: Stir in ½ cup milk with eggs and vanilla. Increase flour to 1½ cups.

Double Chocolate Brownies: Add 1 cup BAKER'S® Real Semi-Sweet Chocolate Chips with the nuts.

Extra Thick Brownies: Bake in 9-inch square pan for 50 minutes.

Rocky Road Brownies: Prepare Brownies as directed. Bake 35 minutes. Immediately sprinkle 2 cups KRAFT® Miniature Marshmallows, 1 cup BAKER'S® Real Semi-Sweet Chocolate Chips and 1 cup coarsely chopped nuts over brownies. Continue baking 3 to 5 minutes or until topping begins to melt together. Cool.

Cream Cheese Brownies: Prepare Brownies as directed using 4 eggs; spread in prepared pan. In same bowl mix 2 (3 oz.) packages PHILADELPHIA BRAND® Cream Cheese, softened, ¼ cup sugar, 1 egg and 2 tablespoons flour. Spoon mixture over brownie batter; swirl with knife to marbelize. Bake 40 minutes.

Cranberry-Orange Muesli Bars

Makes 24 bars

Filling
1 package (12 oz.) OCEAN SPRAY®
    cranberries, fresh or frozen
1 cup granulated sugar
1 teaspoon grated orange peel, optional
1 cup orange juice

Base/Topping
4 cups RALSTON® brand Fruit Muesli with
    Cranberries, crushed to 3 cups
1½ cups all-purpose flour
¾ cup packed brown sugar
1½ teaspoons baking powder
½ teaspoon salt
¾ cup (1½ sticks) margarine or butter, softened

To prepare Filling: In medium saucepan over medium heat combine cranberries, granulated sugar, orange peel, if desired, and orange juice. Cook, stirring frequently, until mixture comes to a boil. Reduce heat; simmer 15 to 18 minutes, stirring frequently. Cool.

To prepare Base/Topping: Preheat oven to 350°F. In large bowl combine cereal, flour, brown sugar, baking powder, salt and margarine. Reserve 1½ cups cereal mixture for topping; set aside. Press remaining cereal mixture firmly and evenly into ungreased 13×9×2-inch baking pan. Bake 10 minutes. Spread cranberry filling evenly over base; sprinkle with reserved cereal mixture. Bake an additional 18 to 20 minutes or until lightly browned.

Frost on the Pumpkin Cookies

Makes about 48 cookies

2 cups all-purpose flour
1 teaspoon baking powder
1 teaspoon ground cinnamon
1/2 teaspoon baking soda
1/2 teaspoon ground nutmeg
1 cup butter, softened
3/4 cup JACK FROST® granulated sugar
3/4 cup JACK FROST® brown sugar (packed)
1 egg
1 cup canned pumpkin
2 teaspoons vanilla
1/2 cup raisins
1/2 cup chopped walnuts
    Cream Cheese Frosting

In small mixing bowl combine flour, baking powder, cinnamon, baking soda and nutmeg. Set aside. In large mixer bowl beat butter for 1 minute. Add granulated sugar and brown sugar. Beat until fluffy. Add egg, pumpkin and vanilla; beat well. Add dry ingredients to beaten mixture; mix until well blended. Stir in raisins and walnuts. Drop by teaspoonfuls 2 inches apart onto greased cookie sheet. Bake in 350°F oven for 10 to 12 minutes. Cool on cookie sheet for 2 minutes, then transfer to wire rack to finish cooling. Frost with Cream Cheese Frosting. Garnish with chopped nuts, if desired.

Cream Cheese Frosting: In medium mixing bowl, beat 3 ounces softened cream cheese, 1/4 cup softened butter and 1 teaspoon vanilla until light and fluffy. Gradually add 2 cups JACK FROST® powdered sugar, beating until smooth.

Chunky Chocolate Cookie Squares

Makes 2 dozen

2 1/2 cups all-purpose flour
1 teaspoon baking soda
1/2 teaspoon salt
3/4 cup butter or margarine, softened
1 cup firmly packed brown sugar
3/4 cup light or dark corn syrup
1 egg
1 teaspoon vanilla
1 cup chopped pecans
1 package (8 oz.) BAKER'S® Semi-Sweet
    Chocolate *or* 2 packages (4 oz. each)
    BAKER'S® GERMAN'S® Sweet Chocolate,
    cut into large chunks

Mix flour, baking soda and salt; set aside. Beat butter and sugar in large bowl of electric mixer at medium speed until light and fluffy. Slowly beat in corn syrup, then egg and vanilla. Beat in flour mixture until blended. Stir in pecans and half of the chocolate. Spread evenly in ungreased 15 1/2 ×10 1/2 ×1-inch jelly roll pan. Sprinkle remaining chocolate on top. Bake at 350°F for 30 minutes, or until lightly browned. Cool on rack. Cut into 2 1/2 -inch squares.

Easy Peanut Butter Chocolate Fudge

Makes about 2 pounds

1 (12-ounce) package peanut butter flavored
    chips
1/4 cup margarine or butter
1 (14-ounce) can EAGLE® Brand Sweetened
    Condensed Milk (NOT evaporated milk)
1/2 cup chopped peanuts, optional
1 (6-ounce) package semi-sweet chocolate chips
    (1 cup)

In heavy saucepan, melt peanut butter chips and *2 tablespoons* margarine with *1 cup* sweetened condensed milk. Remove from heat; stir in peanuts if desired. Spread into wax paper-lined 8-inch square pan. In small heavy saucepan, melt chocolate chips and remaining *2 tablespoons* margarine with remaining sweetened condensed milk. Spread chocolate mixture on top of peanut butter mixture. Chill 2 hours or until firm. Turn fudge onto cutting board; peel off paper and cut into squares. Store loosely covered at room temperature.

Easy Peanut Butter Chocolate Fudge

Desserts

Almond Chocolate Torte with Raspberry Sauce

Makes 10 to 12 servings

2½ cups **BLUE DIAMOND® Blanched Whole Almonds**, lightly toasted
9 squares (1 ounce each) semisweet chocolate
¼ cup butter
6 eggs, beaten
¾ cup sugar
2 tablespoons flour
¼ cup brandy
 Fudge Glaze (recipe follows)
 Raspberry Sauce (recipe follows)

In food processor or blender, process 1 cup of the almonds until finely ground. Generously grease 9-inch round cake pan; sprinkle with 2 tablespoons ground almonds. In top of double boiler, melt chocolate and butter over simmering water, blending thoroughly; cool slightly. In large bowl, beat eggs and sugar. Gradually beat in chocolate mixture. Add flour, remaining ground almonds and brandy; mix well. Pour batter into prepared pan. Bake in preheated 350°F oven 25 minutes or until toothpick inserted into center comes out almost clean. Let cool in pan on wire rack 10 minutes. Loosen edge; remove from pan. Cool completely on wire rack. Prepare Fudge Glaze. Place torte on wire rack over sheet of waxed paper. Pour Fudge Glaze over torte, spreading over top and sides with spatula. Carefully transfer torte to serving plate; let glaze set. Prepare Raspberry Sauce; set aside. Arrange remaining 1½ cups whole almonds, points toward center, in circle around outer edge of torte. Working towards center, repeat circles, overlapping almonds slightly. To serve, pour small amount of Raspberry Sauce on each serving plate; top with slice of torte.

Fudge Glaze: In small saucepan, combine 6 tablespoons water and 3 tablespoons sugar. Simmer over low heat until sugar dissolves. Stir in 3 squares (1 ounce each) semisweet chocolate and 1 tablespoon brandy. Heat, stirring occasionally, until chocolate melts and glaze coats back of spoon.

Raspberry Sauce: In food processor or blender, puree 2 packages (10 ounces each) thawed frozen raspberries. Strain raspberry puree through a fine sieve to remove seeds. Stir in sugar to taste.

Quick Rumtopf

Makes 2 quarts

1 can (16 oz.) **DEL MONTE® Yellow Cling Sliced Peaches**
1 can (16 oz.) **DEL MONTE® Bartlett Pear Halves**
1 can (15½ oz.) **DEL MONTE® Pineapple Chunks**
1 can (11 oz.) **DEL MONTE® Mandarin Oranges**
1 cup rum
1 cinnamon stick
½ cup **DEL MONTE® Seedless Raisins**

Drain fruit reserving syrup in medium saucepan. Add rum and cinnamon stick to reserved syrup. Bring to a boil, stirring occasionally. Cool. Layer fruit and raisins in rumtopf pot or large jars. Pour syrup mixture over fruit. Refrigerate. Allow 1 week to mellow. Serve as fruit compote or on ice cream or pound cake.

Almond Chocolate Torte with Raspberry Sauce

Almond Chocolate Torte with
Raspberry Sauce

Torte:
1 cup Blue Diamond Blanched
Whole Almonds, toasted
sweet chocolate

Charlotte Russe

Charlotte Russe

Makes 10 servings

2 packages (4-serving size each) *or* 1 package
    (8-serving size) **JELL-O®** Brand Gelatin,
    any red flavor
2 cups boiling water
1 quart vanilla ice cream, softened
12 ladyfingers, split
    COOL-WHIP® Whipped Topping, thawed
    (optional)
    Fresh raspberries (optional)
    Mint leaves (optional)

Dissolve gelatin in boiling water. Spoon in ice cream,
stirring until melted and smooth. Chill until
thickened.

Trim about 1 inch off one end of each ladyfinger;
reserve trimmed ends for snacking or other use.
Place ladyfingers, cut ends down, around side of 8-
inch springform pan. Spoon gelatin mixture into
pan. Chill until firm, about 3 hours. Remove side of
pan. Garnish with whipped topping, raspberries and
mint leaves, if desired.

Preparation time: 20 minutes
Chill time: 3 hours

New England Maple Apple Pie

Makes one 9-inch pie

1 (9-inch) unbaked pastry shell
2 pounds all-purpose apples, pared, cored and
    thinly sliced (about 6 cups)
1/2 cup plus 2 tablespoons unsifted flour
1/2 cup **CARY'S®, VERMONT MAPLE
    ORCHARDS** or **MACDONALD'S** Pure
    Maple Syrup
2 tablespoons margarine or butter, melted
1/4 cup firmly packed light brown sugar
1 teaspoon ground cinnamon
1/3 cup cold margarine or butter
1/2 cup chopped nuts

Place rack in lowest position in oven; preheat oven to
400°F. In large bowl, combine apples and *2 tablespoons*
flour. Combine syrup and melted margarine. Pour
over apples; mix well. Turn into pastry shell. In
medium bowl, combine remaining *1/2 cup* flour, sugar
and cinnamon; cut in cold margarine until crumbly.
Add nuts; sprinkle over apples. Bake 10 minutes.
Reduce oven temperature to 375°F; bake 35 minutes longer
or until golden brown. Cool slightly. Serve warm.

German Sweet Chocolate Cake

Makes about 10 servings

1 package (4 oz.) **BAKER'S® GERMAN'S®**
    Sweet Chocolate
½ cup boiling water
1 cup (2 sticks) butter or margarine
2 cups sugar
4 eggs, separated
1 teaspoon vanilla
2 cups all-purpose flour
1 teaspoon baking soda
½ teaspoon salt
1 cup buttermilk
    Coconut-Pecan Frosting (recipe follows)

Line bottoms of three 9-inch layer pans with waxed paper. Melt chocolate in water; cool. Beat butter and sugar. Beat in egg yolks. Stir in vanilla and chocolate. Mix flour, baking soda and salt. Beat into chocolate mixture alternately with buttermilk. Beat egg whites until stiff peaks form; fold into batter. Pour into prepared pans. Bake at 350°F for 30 minutes or until cake springs back when lightly pressed in center. Cool 15 minutes; remove and cool on racks. Spread Coconut-Pecan Frosting between layers and over top of cake.

Coconut-Pecan Frosting: Combine 1½ cups (12 fl. oz.) evaporated milk, 1½ cups sugar, 4 slightly beaten egg yolks, ¾ cup butter and 1½ teaspoons vanilla in saucepan. Cook and stir over medium heat until thickened. Remove from heat. Stir in 2 cups BAKER'S® ANGEL FLAKE® Coconut and 1½ cups chopped pecans. Cool until thick enough to spread. Makes 4¼ cups.

Holiday Creme Chantilly

Makes about 8 servings

2 cups milk
½ cup sugar
⅓ cup all-purpose flour
1 envelope unflavored gelatin
¼ teaspoon salt
2 eggs
2 egg yolks
¼ to ⅓ cup dark rum
1 cup heavy whipping cream
½ cup finely chopped **DIAMOND®** Walnuts
    Orange Walnut Sauce (recipe follows)

In medium saucepan, scald milk over low heat. In medium bowl, combine sugar, flour, gelatin and salt. Add eggs and egg yolks; beat well. Stir in hot milk. Return to saucepan and cook over medium-low heat, stirring constantly, until mixture thickens and just reaches a boil. Remove from heat; stir in rum. Set pan in bowl of ice water; cool thoroughly, stirring occasionally. In medium bowl, beat cream until stiff peaks form. Fold cream and walnuts into the cooled custard mixture. Spoon into individual serving dishes or individual oiled molds. Chill thoroughly. At serving time, spoon Orange Walnut Sauce over Chantilly.

Orange Walnut Sauce

2 to 3 oranges
½ cup sugar
½ teaspoon cornstarch
1 tablespoon lemon juice
¼ cup coarsely chopped **DIAMOND®** Walnuts

With vegetable peeler, remove the outer colored layer of oranges. Cut enough of orange peel into slivers with sharp knife to measure 3 tablespoons. Squeeze juice from oranges to measure 1 cup. In small saucepan, simmer juice and slivers over low heat 5 minutes. In small bowl, combine sugar and cornstarch; blend into hot mixture. Cook and stir over medium heat until mixture boils and thickens. Add lemon juice; cool. Add walnuts just before serving. Makes about ¾ cup sauce.

Holiday Creme Chantilly

Easy Chocolate Cheesecake

Easy Chocolate Cheesecake

Makes 8 servings

  2 packages (4 oz. each) **BAKER'S®**
     GERMAN'S® Sweet Chocolate
$1/3$ cup heavy cream
  2 eggs
$2/3$ cup corn syrup
$1^1/2$ teaspoons vanilla
  2 packages (8 oz. each) cream cheese, cut into
     cubes
     Crumb Crust (recipe follows)

Microwave $1^1/2$ packages (6 oz.) of the chocolate and the cream in microwavable bowl at HIGH 2 minutes. *Stir until chocolate is completely melted.* Blend eggs, corn syrup and vanilla in blender until smooth. With blender running, gradually add cream cheese; blend until smooth. Add chocolate mixture; blend. Pour into crust. Bake at 325°F for 45 minutes or until set. Cool on rack. Cover; chill. Melt remaining chocolate; drizzle over top.

Crumb Crust: In 9-inch pie plate or 9×3-inch springform pan, combine $1^3/4$ cups chocolate cookie or graham cracker crumbs, 2 tablespoons sugar and $1/3$ cup butter or margarine, melted, until well mixed. Press evenly in pie plate or on bottom and $1^1/4$ inches up side of springform pan.

Range Top: Heat chocolate and cream in saucepan over very low heat, stirring until chocolate is melted. Continue as above.

Butterscotch Apple Squares

Makes 12 servings

$1/4$ cup margarine or butter
$1^1/2$ cups graham cracker crumbs
  2 small all-purpose apples, pared and chopped
     (about $1^1/4$ cups)
  1 (6-ounce) package butterscotch flavored chips
  1 (14-ounce) can **EAGLE®** Brand Sweetened
     Condensed Milk (NOT evaporated milk)
  1 ($3^1/2$-ounce) can flaked coconut ($1^1/3$ cups)
  1 cup chopped nuts

Preheat oven to 350°F (325° for glass dish). In 13×9-inch baking pan, melt margarine in oven. Sprinkle crumbs evenly over margarine; top with apples. In heavy saucepan, over medium heat, melt chips with sweetened condensed milk. Pour butterscotch mixture evenly over apples. Top with coconut and nuts; press down firmly. Bake 25 to 30 minutes or until lightly browned. Cool. Garnish as desired. Refrigerate leftovers.

Microwave: In 12×7-inch baking dish, melt margarine on 100% power (high) 1 minute. Sprinkle crumbs evenly over margarine; top with apples. In 1-quart glass measure, cook chips with sweetened condensed milk on 75% power (medium-high) 2 to 3 minutes. Mix well. Pour butterscotch mixture evenly over apples. Top with coconut and nuts. Press down firmly. Cook on 100% power (high) 8 to 9 minutes. Proceed as above.

Creamy Macaroon Indulgence

Makes 4 servings

$1^1/2$ cups cold milk
  1 cup ($1/2$ pint) sour cream
  2 tablespoons almond liqueur*
  1 package (4-serving size) **JELL-O®** Instant
     Pudding and Pie Filling, any flavor
$1/2$ cup crumbled macaroon cookies

Mix milk, sour cream and liqueur in small bowl until smooth. Add pudding mix. Beat with wire whisk until well blended, 1 to 2 minutes. Spoon $1/2$ the pudding mixture into dessert dishes. Sprinkle crumbled macaroons evenly over pudding. Top with remaining pudding mixture. Chill. Garnish with additional cookies, if desired.

Preparation time: 15 minutes

$*1/4$ teaspoon almond extract may be substituted for the almond liqueur.

Christmas Tree Poke Cake

Makes 24 servings

2 packages (2-layer size each) white cake mix
1 package (4-serving size) JELL-O® Brand
    Gelatin, Strawberry Flavor
1 package (4-serving size) JELL-O® Brand
    Gelatin, Lime Flavor
2 cups boiling water
2²/₃ cups (7 oz.) BAKER'S® ANGEL FLAKE®
    Coconut
Green food coloring
5¼ cups (12 oz.) COOL WHIP® Whipped
    Topping, thawed
Assorted gumdrops (optional)
Peppermint candies (optional)
Red string licorice (optional)

Prepare 1 cake mix as directed on package. Pour batter into greased and floured 9-inch square pan. Bake at 325°F for 50 to 55 minutes or until cake tester inserted in center comes out clean. Cool 10 minutes. Remove from pan; finish cooling on rack. Repeat with remaining cake mix.

Place cake layers, top sides up, in 2 clean 9-inch square cake pans. Pierce cakes with large fork at ½-inch intervals. Dissolve each flavor of gelatin separately in 1 cup of the boiling water. Carefully pour strawberry flavor gelatin over 1 cake layer and lime flavor gelatin over second cake layer. Chill 3 hours.

Toast ⅓ cup of the coconut; set aside. Tint remaining coconut with green food coloring. Dip 1 cake pan in warm water 10 seconds; unmold. Place right side up on large serving plate or cutting board. Cut cake as shown in Diagram 1. Arrange pieces as shown in Christmas tree shape (Diagram 2), using small amount of whipped topping to hold pieces together. Top with about 1½ cups of the whipped topping. Unmold second cake layer; cut into pieces as shown in Diagram 1. Place pieces on first layer. Use remaining whipped topping to frost entire cake.

Sprinkle trunk of tree with toasted coconut. Sprinkle remaining cake with green coconut. Decorate with gumdrops, peppermint candies and string licorice, if desired. Chill until ready to serve.

Preparation time: 30 minutes
Chill time: 3 hours

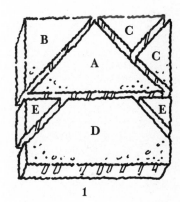

1

Christmas Tree Poke Cake

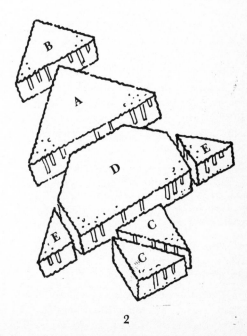

2

Fruitcake Bars (left), Fruitcake-in-a-Can (center), Chocolate Fruitcake (right)

Ever-so-Easy Fruitcake

Makes one 10-inch cake

2½ cups unsifted flour
 1 teaspoon baking soda
 2 eggs, slightly beaten
 1 jar NONE SUCH® Ready-to-Use Mincemeat
      (Regular *or* Brandy & Rum)
 1 (14-ounce) can EAGLE® Brand Sweetened
      Condensed Milk (NOT evaporated milk)
 2 cups (1 pound) mixed candied fruit
 1 cup coarsely chopped nuts

Preheat oven to 300°F. Grease and flour 10-inch
fluted tube pan. Combine flour and baking soda; set
aside. In large bowl, combine remaining ingredients;
blend in dry ingredients. Pour batter into prepared
pan. Bake 1 hour and 45 to 50 minutes or until
wooden pick comes out clean. Cool 15 minutes. Turn
out of pan. Garnish as desired.

Tip: To substitute condensed mincemeat for ready-
to-use mincemeat, crumble 2 (9-ounce) packages
NONE SUCH® Condensed Mincemeat into small
saucepan; add 1½ cups water. Boil briskly 1 minute.
Cool. Proceed as above.

Chocolate Fruitcake: Prepare fruitcake batter as
above, adding 3 (1-ounce) squares unsweetened
chocolate, melted. For glaze, melt 3 (1-ounce)
squares semi-sweet chocolate with 2 tablespoons
margarine or butter. Spoon over fruitcake.

Fruitcake-in-a-Can: Grease three 1-pound coffee
cans; fill each can with about 2⅔ cups batter. Bake 1
hour and 20 to 25 minutes.

Fruitcake Bars: Grease 15×10-inch jellyroll pan;
spread batter evenly in pan. Bake 40 to 45 minutes.
Cool. Glaze if desired. Makes about 4 dozen bars.

Lemon Cheesecake Squares

Makes 18 servings

1¼ cups (18 to 19) shortbread cookie crumbs
 ⅓ cup ground almonds
 3 tablespoons PARKAY® Margarine, melted
 2 tablespoons sugar
 1 6-oz. container frozen lemonade concentrate,
      thawed
 3 8-oz. pkgs. PHILADELPHIA BRAND®
      Cream Cheese, softened
 1 cup sour cream
 1 3½-oz. pkg. JELL-O® Brand Lemon Flavor
      Instant Pudding and Pie Filling
 2 cups COOL WHIP® Whipped Topping,
      thawed

Preheat oven to 350°F. Stir together crumbs,
almonds, margarine and sugar in small bowl; press
onto bottom of 13×9-inch baking pan. Bake 10
minutes. Cool. Gradually add lemonade concentrate
to cream cheese in large mixing bowl, mixing at low
speed with electric mixer until well blended. Add
sour cream and pudding mix; beat 1 minute. Fold in
whipped topping; pour over crust. Freeze until firm.
Cut into squares. Garnish with fresh berries and
mint, if desired.

Preparation time: 15 minutes plus freezing

Festive Eggnog Cake

Makes 16 servings

Cake
1 1/3 cups sugar
1/2 cup LAND O LAKES® Sweet Cream
  Butter
2 eggs
2 1/2 cups all-purpose flour
1/2 cup chopped blanched almonds
1 1/4 cups milk
1 tablespoon baking powder
1 teaspoon nutmeg
1/2 teaspoon rum extract

Glaze
1 cup powdered sugar
2 tablespoons LAND O LAKES® Sweet Cream
  Butter
4 to 5 teaspoons milk
1/4 teaspoon rum extract

  Whole almonds
  Candied cherries

Heat oven to 350°F. For cake, in large mixer bowl combine sugar and butter. Beat at medium speed, scraping bowl often, until well mixed (2 to 3 minutes). Add eggs; continue beating until light and fluffy (3 to 5 minutes). Add remaining cake ingredients. Reduce to low speed; continue beating, scraping bowl often, until well mixed (2 to 3 minutes). Pour into greased and floured 10-inch fluted tube pan. Bake for 45 to 55 minutes or until wooden pick inserted near center comes out clean. Cool in pan 10 minutes. Loosen edge; remove from pan and cool completely. In small bowl combine all glaze ingredients until smooth. Drizzle over cake; garnish with whole almonds and candied cherry halves. Store tightly covered.

Heath® Bar Cheesecake

Makes 10 to 12 servings

Crust
1 3/4 cups vanilla wafer crumbs
2 tablespoons sugar
1/3 cup margarine, melted

Filling
3 (8 oz.) packages cream cheese, softened
1 cup sugar
3 eggs
1 cup sour cream
1 1/2 teaspoons vanilla
5 (1.2-oz.) HEATH® Bars, crushed

Preheat oven to 350°F. Combine crust ingredients; press into bottom and 1 1/2 inches up side of 9-inch springform pan. Refrigerate.

In large mixer bowl, beat cream cheese with sugar at medium speed until fluffy. Add eggs, 1 at a time, beating well after each addition. Beat in sour cream and vanilla; blend until smooth. Spoon half of the filling over prepared crust. Sprinkle half of the HEATH® Bars over the filling; cover with remaining filling. Bake 1 hour or until cheesecake is just firm when pan is tapped gently. Cool completely in pan on wire rack. Sprinkle remaining HEATH® Bars over the top. Refrigerate until chilled.

Pumpkin Jingle Bars

Makes about 3 dozen

3/4 cup MIRACLE WHIP® Salad Dressing
1 two-layer spice cake mix
1 16-oz. can pumpkin
3 eggs
  Confectioners' sugar
  Vanilla frosting
  Red and green gum drops, sliced

Mix first 4 ingredients in large bowl at medium speed of electric mixer until well blended. Pour into greased 15 1/2×10 1/2×1-inch jelly roll pan. Bake at 350°F, 18 to 20 minutes or until edges pull away from sides of pan. Cool. Sprinkle with sugar. Cut into bars. Decorate with frosting and gum drops.

Preparation time: 5 minutes
Cooking time: 20 minutes

Pumpkin Jingle Bars

Cranmallow Cheesecake

Makes 10 to 12 servings

¾ cup graham cracker crumbs
½ cup finely chopped macadamia nuts
¼ cup **PARKAY®** Margarine, melted
2 tablespoons sugar
1 envelope unflavored gelatin
¼ cup cold water
2 8-oz. pkgs. **PHILADELPHIA BRAND®** Cream Cheese, softened
1 7-oz. jar **KRAFT®** Marshmallow Creme
1 16-oz. can whole berry cranberry sauce
1 cup whipping cream, whipped

Combine crumbs, nuts, margarine and sugar; press onto bottom of 9-inch springform pan. Bake at 350°F, 10 minutes; cool. In small saucepan, soften gelatin in water; stir over low heat until dissolved. Mix cream cheese and marshmallow creme at medium speed with electric mixer until well blended. Gradually add gelatin mixture and cranberry sauce, mixing until well blended. Fold in whipped cream; pour over crust. Chill until firm. Garnish with fresh cranberries and mint sprigs, if desired.

Variation: *Substitute ½ cup finely chopped walnuts for macadamia nuts.*

Cranmallow Cheesecake

Gingerbread Upside-Down Cake

Makes 8 to 10 servings

1 can (20 oz.) **DOLE®** Pineapple Slices
½ cup margarine, softened
1 cup brown sugar, packed
10 maraschino cherries
1 egg
½ cup dark molasses
1½ cups all-purpose flour
1 teaspoon baking soda
1 teaspoon ground ginger
½ teaspoon ground cinnamon
½ teaspoon salt

Preheat oven to 350°F. Drain pineapple; reserve ½ cup syrup. In 10-inch cast iron skillet, melt ¼ cup margarine. Remove from heat. Add ½ cup brown sugar and stir until blended. Arrange pineapple slices in skillet. Place 1 cherry in center of each slice. In large mixer bowl, beat remaining ¼ cup margarine and ½ cup brown sugar until light and fluffy. Beat in egg and molasses. In small bowl, combine flour, baking soda, ginger, cinnamon and salt.

In small saucepan, bring reserved pineapple syrup to boil. Add dry ingredients to creamed mixture alternately with hot syrup. Spread evenly over pineapple in skillet. Bake in preheated oven 30 to 40 minutes or until wooden pick inserted into center comes out clean. Let stand in skillet on wire rack 5 minutes. Invert onto serving plate.

Mocha Walnut Tart

Makes one 9-inch pie

1 (9-inch) unbaked pastry shell
2 (1-ounce) squares unsweetened chocolate
¼ cup margarine or butter
1 (14-ounce) can **EAGLE®** Brand Sweetened Condensed Milk (**NOT** evaporated milk)
¼ cup water
2 eggs, well beaten
¼ cup coffee-flavored liqueur
1 teaspoon vanilla extract
⅛ teaspoon salt
1 cup walnuts, toasted and chopped

Preheat oven to 350°F. In medium saucepan, over low heat, melt chocolate and margarine. Stir in sweetened condensed milk, water and eggs; *mix well.* Remove from heat; stir in liqueur, vanilla and salt. Pour into pastry shell; top with walnuts. Bake 40 to 45 minutes or until center is set. Cool. Serve warm or chilled. Garnish as desired. Refrigerate leftovers.

Creole Lemon Cake

Creole Lemon Cake

Makes one 10-inch cake

  2 cups butter or margarine, softened
  2 cups granulated sugar
  6 eggs
  1/2 cup lemon juice
  3 tablespoons grated lemon peel
3 3/4 cups all-purpose flour
  2 teaspoons baking powder
  4 cups coarsely chopped **DIAMOND®** Walnuts
2 1/2 cups **SUN-MAID®** Raisins or Golden Raisins
     Powdered sugar, for garnish

In large bowl, cream butter and granulated sugar. Add eggs, one at a time, beating well after each addition. Stir in lemon juice and peel. In another large bowl, combine remaining ingredients, except powdered sugar; gradually stir into butter mixture, mixing just until blended. Spoon batter into well-greased and floured 10-inch tube pan; let stand 10 minutes. Bake in preheated 325°F oven 1 hour and 45 minutes or until browned and pick inserted near center comes out clean. Let cool in pan on wire rack 15 minutes. Loosen edges and remove from pan. Cool completely on wire rack. Wrap; let stand a day before slicing. Before serving, dust with powdered sugar, if desired.

Note: Cake can be wrapped in brandy-soaked cheesecloth and stored in covered container in cool, dry place 1 to 2 weeks.

Chocolate Applesauce Cake

Makes about 12 servings

2 1/2 cups all-purpose flour
  1/3 cup unsweetened cocoa
  2 teaspoons baking soda
  3/4 teaspoon salt
  3/4 cup shortening
1 3/4 cups sugar
  2 eggs
1 1/2 teaspoons vanilla
1 1/2 cups sweetened applesauce
  1/2 cup buttermilk

In small bowl, combine flour, cocoa, baking soda and salt. In large bowl, cream shortening and sugar. Beat in eggs and vanilla. In small bowl, combine applesauce and buttermilk; mix well. Add dry ingredients to creamed mixture alternately with applesauce mixture; mix until well blended. Pour batter into greased 13×9×2-inch pan. Bake in preheated 350°F oven 35 to 40 minutes or until toothpick inserted into center comes out clean. Cool completely in pan on wire rack. Serve plain or top with your favorite frosting.

Favorite recipe from **Western New York Apple Growers Association, Inc.**

Traditional Pumpkin Pie

Traditional Pumpkin Pie

Makes one 9-inch pie

1 (9-inch) unbaked pastry shell
1 (16-ounce) can pumpkin (2 cups)
1 (14-ounce) can EAGLE® Brand Sweetened
    Condensed Milk (NOT evaporated milk)
2 eggs
1 teaspoon ground cinnamon
1/2 teaspoon ground ginger
1/2 teaspoon ground nutmeg
1/2 teaspoon salt

Place rack in lowest position in oven; preheat oven to 425°F. In large mixer bowl, combine all ingredients except pastry shell; mix well. Pour into pastry shell. Bake 15 minutes. *Reduce oven temperature to 350°F;* bake 35 to 40 minutes longer or until knife inserted near edge comes out clean. Cool. Garnish as desired. Refrigerate leftovers.

Optional Toppings

Sour Cream Topping: In medium bowl, combine 1 1/2 cups BORDEN® or MEADOW GOLD® Sour Cream, 2 tablespoons sugar and 1 teaspoon vanilla extract. After 30 minutes of baking, spread evenly over top of pie; bake 10 minutes longer. Garnish as desired.

Streusel Topping: In medium bowl, combine 1/2 cup firmly packed light brown sugar and 1/2 cup unsifted flour; cut in 1/4 cup cold margarine or butter until crumbly. Stir in 1/4 cup chopped nuts. After 30 minutes of baking, sprinkle on top of pie; bake 10 minutes longer.

Cinnamon Crisp Plum Pudding

Makes 8 to 10 servings

2 cups KEEBLER® Cinnamon Crisp Graham
    Cracker Crumbs (about 15 large crackers)
1 1/4 teaspoons baking soda
1/2 teaspoon salt
1/4 teaspoon ground ginger
1/4 teaspoon ground cloves
1/2 cup shortening
1/2 cup packed brown sugar
2 eggs
1/2 cup water
1 can (16 ounces) purple plums in heavy syrup,
    drained, pitted and chopped (syrup
    reserved)
1 cup golden raisins
1/2 cup chopped walnuts
Plum Sauce (recipe follows)

Stir together Cinnamon Crisp Cracker Crumbs, baking soda, salt, ginger and cloves; set aside. Cream shortening with brown sugar until fluffy. Beat in eggs 1 at a time. Add crumb mixture alternately with water to sugar mixture, beating well after each addition. Stir in chopped plums, raisins, and walnuts. If mixture is dry, stir in more water 1 tablespoon at at time. Pour batter into well-greased 5- or 6-cup kugelhopf or Bundt® pan. Bake in preheated 375°F oven 40 to 50 minutes or until wooden pick inserted near center comes out clean. Loosen edges of plum pudding; immediately turn out of pan onto serving platter. Spoon Plum Sauce over slices of pudding.

Plum Sauce: Combine plum syrup (about 1 cup), 1/4 cup granulated sugar and 2 tablespoons cornstarch in small saucepan. Cook over medium heat, stirring constantly, until thickened, about 5 minutes. Stir in 1 tablespoon lemon juice or brandy.

Raspberry Pear Cheesecake

Makes 6 to 8 servings

1 (6½- to 8-inch diameter) prepared plain
  cheesecake
1 (10-ounce) package frozen raspberries in
  syrup, thawed
2 teaspoons cornstarch
3 to 4 canned pear halves, well drained
  Fresh raspberries, if desired
½ ounce semi-sweet chocolate
½ teaspoon solid shortening

Combine frozen raspberries in syrup and cornstarch
in a small saucepan. Stir to dissolve cornstarch. Over
medium heat, bring to a boil and cook just until
clear and thickened, stirring constantly. Cool for 10
minutes. Spoon ⅓ cup raspberry sauce on top of
cheesecake. Cut pear halves in half lengthwise.
Arrange pears spoke-fashion on top of sauce. Garnish
with fresh raspberries, if desired. Melt chocolate with
shortening. Drizzle over pears. Cut into wedges and
serve with remaining raspberry sauce.

Canned Pears

4 pounds pears
3½ cups water
1¾ cups sugar
3 tablespoons bottled lemon juice
6 KERR® pint jars *or* 3 KERR® quart jars (with
  bands and lids)

Peel, core and halve pears lengthwise. In 6- to 8-
quart saucepan, combine water, sugar and lemon
juice. Over medium-high heat, bring to a boil. Add
pears and return to a boil. Remove from heat.
Immediately fill jars with pears and syrup, leaving
½-inch headspace. Carefully run a non-metallic
utensil down inside of jars to remove trapped air
bubbles. Wipe jar tops and threads clean. Place hot
lids on jars and screw bands on firmly. Process in
Boiling Water Canner 20 minutes for pint jars, 25
minutes for quart jars. Makes 6 pints or 3 quarts.

*Notes: For smaller yield, halve ingredients. Processing times
and other directions remain the same.*

*Processing times must be increased for altitudes higher than
1000 feet. For altitudes between 1001-3000 feet add 5
minutes; 3001-6000 feet add 10 minutes; 6001-8000 feet add
15 minutes; 8001-10,000 feet add 20 minutes.*

Raspberry Pear Cheesecake

French Silk Mint Pie

Makes 1 pie

1 **KEEBLER®** Chocolate-flavored Ready Crust
   pie crust
2 cups powdered sugar, sifted
1/2 lb. unsalted butter, softened
4 eggs*
4 (1-ounce) squares unsweetened chocolate,
   melted and cooled
1/4 teaspoon mint extract
1/4 teaspoon vanilla extract
   Fresh mint and maraschino cherries, for
   garnish

Beat sugar with butter in large bowl until smooth.
Add eggs, 1 at a time, beating well after each
addition. Add melted chocolate; stir in extracts. Mix
well; pour into crumb crust. Refrigerate until firm.
Just before serving, garnish with mint and cherries.
Cut into small pieces.

Use clean, uncracked eggs.

French Silk Mint Pie

Winterfruit Cobbler

Makes 6 servings

Filling
2 cups **SUN-MAID®** Raisins
2 cups fresh or frozen cranberries
3/4 cup sugar
2 teaspoons cornstarch
1/2 teaspoon ground allspice
1 cup orange juice

Topping
1 cup all-purpose flour
2 tablespoons sugar
2 teaspoons baking powder
1/4 teaspoon salt
1/4 cup butter or margarine
1/2 cup milk
   Sugar
   Ground cinnamon

To prepare Filling: In medium saucepan, combine
raisins, cranberries, sugar, cornstarch and allspice.
Gradually stir in orange juice. Bring to boil over high
heat; reduce heat to low and simmer, stirring until
cranberries begin to pop and mixture thickens
slightly. Pour into shallow 1 1/2-quart baking dish.

To prepare Topping: In small bowl, combine flour,
sugar, baking powder and salt. Cut in butter until
mixture resembles coarse meal. Mix in milk lightly
with fork. Drop spoonfuls of batter over filling;
sprinkle lightly with additional sugar mixed with a
little cinnamon. Bake in preheated 400°F oven about
25 minutes or until golden. Serve warm with ice
cream or whipping cream.

Pumpkin Orange Cheesecake

Makes one 9-inch cheesecake

1 1/2 cups gingersnap cookie crumbs (32 cookies)
1/4 cup margarine or butter, melted
3 (8-ounce) packages cream cheese, softened
1 (14-ounce) can **EAGLE®** Brand Sweetened
   Condensed Milk (**NOT** evaporated milk)
1 (16-ounce) can pumpkin (2 cups)
2 eggs
3 tablespoons orange-flavored liqueur *or* orange
   juice
1 teaspoon pumpkin pie spice
1/4 teaspoon salt
   Whipped topping or whipped cream

Preheat oven to 300°F. Combine crumbs and margarine. Press firmly on bottom and halfway up side of 9-inch springform pan. In large mixer bowl, beat cheese until fluffy. Gradually beat in sweetened condensed milk until smooth. Add remaining ingredients except whipped topping; mix well. Pour into prepared pan. Bake 1 hour and 15 minutes or until cake springs back when lightly touched (center will be slightly soft). Cool to room temperature. Chill. Serve with whipped topping. Garnish as desired. Refrigerate leftovers.

Plum Pudding Pie (top), Pumpkin & Cream Cheese Tart with Cranberry-Orange Topping (bottom)

Pumpkin & Cream Cheese Tart with Cranberry-Orange Topping

Makes 10 to 12 servings

Pie crust mix for single 9-inch crust
4 packages (3 ounces each) cream cheese, softened
¾ cup packed brown sugar
2 eggs
1 teaspoon ground cinnamon
¼ teaspoon ground nutmeg
1 teaspoon grated orange peel
1 can (16 ounces) solid pack pumpkin
1 can (16 ounces) OCEAN SPRAY® Whole Berry Cranberry Sauce
Glazed Orange Slices (recipe follows)

Prepare pie crust mix according to package directions. Press dough onto bottom and 1½ inches up side of ungreased 9-inch springform pan; set aside. In large bowl, beat cream cheese and sugar until light and fluffy. Beat in eggs, 1 at a time. Stir in cinnamon, nutmeg, orange peel and pumpkin until smooth and well blended. Pour into pastry-lined pan; spread evenly. Place in preheated 425°F oven; *immediately reduce oven temperature to 350°F.* Bake 35 minutes or until center is almost set. Cool completely in pan on wire rack. Spread whole berry cranberry sauce on top. Arrange Glazed Orange Slices in overlapping ring on top of cranberry sauce. Refrigerate until serving time. Remove side of springform pan before serving.

Glazed Orange Slices: In medium skillet, combine 1 cup granulated sugar and ¼ cup water. Bring to a boil over medium heat; boil 1 minute. Add 12 thin orange slices. Cook over low heat, turning frequently, 5 minutes or until slices are almost translucent.

Plum Pudding Pie

Makes 8 servings

⅓ cup plus 2 tablespoons KAHLÚA®
½ cup golden raisins
½ cup chopped pitted dates
⅓ cup chopped candied cherries
½ cup chopped walnuts
⅓ cup dark corn syrup
½ teaspoon pumpkin pie spice
¼ cup butter or margarine, softened
¼ cup packed brown sugar
2 tablespoons all-purpose flour
¼ teaspoon salt
2 eggs, slightly beaten
1 (9-inch) unbaked pie shell
1 cup whipping cream
Maraschino cherries (optional)

In medium bowl, combine ⅓ cup of the KAHLÚA®, the raisins, dates and cherries; mix well. Cover; let stand 1 to 4 hours. Stir in walnuts, corn syrup and spice. In large bowl, cream butter, sugar, flour and salt. Stir in eggs. Add fruit mixture; blend well. Pour into unbaked pie shell. Bake in preheated 350°F oven 35 minutes or until filling is firm and crust is golden. Cool completely on wire rack. When ready to serve, in small bowl, beat whipping cream with remaining 2 tablespoons KAHLÚA® just until soft peaks form. Spoon cream into pastry bag fitted with large star tip and pipe decoratively on top. If desired, garnish with maraschino cherries.

Acknowledgments

*The publishers would like to thank the companies
and organizations listed below for the use
of their recipes in this book.*

American Egg Board
Blue Diamond Growers
Borden, Inc.
Campbell Soup Company
Checkerboard Kitchens, Ralston Purina
  Company
Chef Paul Prudhomme's Magic Seasoning
  Blends™
Del Monte Corporation
Dole Packaged Foods Company
Domino® Sugars
Durkee-French Foods, A Division of Reckitt
  & Colman Inc.
Heinz U.S.A.
Hellmann's® Mayonnaise
The J. M. Smucker Company
Keebler Company
Kellogg Company
Kerr Corporation
Kikkoman International Inc.

Knorr® Soup and Recipe Mix
Kraft General Foods, Inc.
Land O' Lakes, Inc.
Lawry's Foods, Inc.
Maidstone Wine & Spirits, Inc.
McIlhenny Company
National Pork Producers Council
National Turkey Federation
Norseland Foods, Inc.
Ocean Spray Cranberries, Inc.
The Procter & Gamble Company, Inc.
The Quaker Oats Company
Refined Sugars Incorporated
StarKist Seafood Company
Sun-Diamond Growers of California
Swift-Eckrich, Inc.
Thomas J. Lipton, Inc.
Western New York Apple Growers
  Association, Inc.
Wisconsin Milk Marketing Board

Photo Credits

*The publishers would like to thank the companies
and organizations listed below for the use
of their photographs in this book.*

Blue Diamond Growers
Borden, Inc.
Campbell Soup Company
Checkerboard Kitchens, Ralston Purina
  Company
Del Monte Corporation
Dole Packaged Foods Company
Heinz U.S.A.
Hellmann's® Mayonnaise
Keebler Company
Kellogg Company
Kerr Corporation

Kikkoman International Inc.
Knorr® Soup and Recipe Mix
Kraft General Foods, Inc.
Land O' Lakes, Inc.
Lawry's Foods, Inc.
Maidstone Wine & Spirits, Inc.
The Procter & Gamble Company, Inc.
StarKist Seafood Company
Sun-Diamond Growers of California
Swift-Eckrich, Inc.
Thomas J. Lipton, Inc.

Index